WAITING ON FOREVER

Portraits of Dogs Waiting For Their Forever Home

Photographs by J. Jay Sullivan

Taken At
Save A Dog Rescue
Sudbury, Massachusetts
saveadog.org

All Images © Jay Sullivan 2014

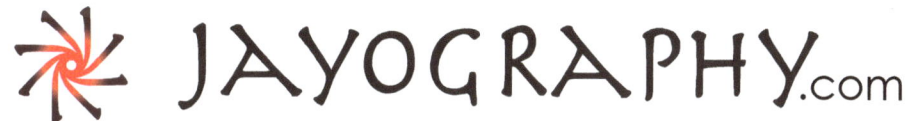

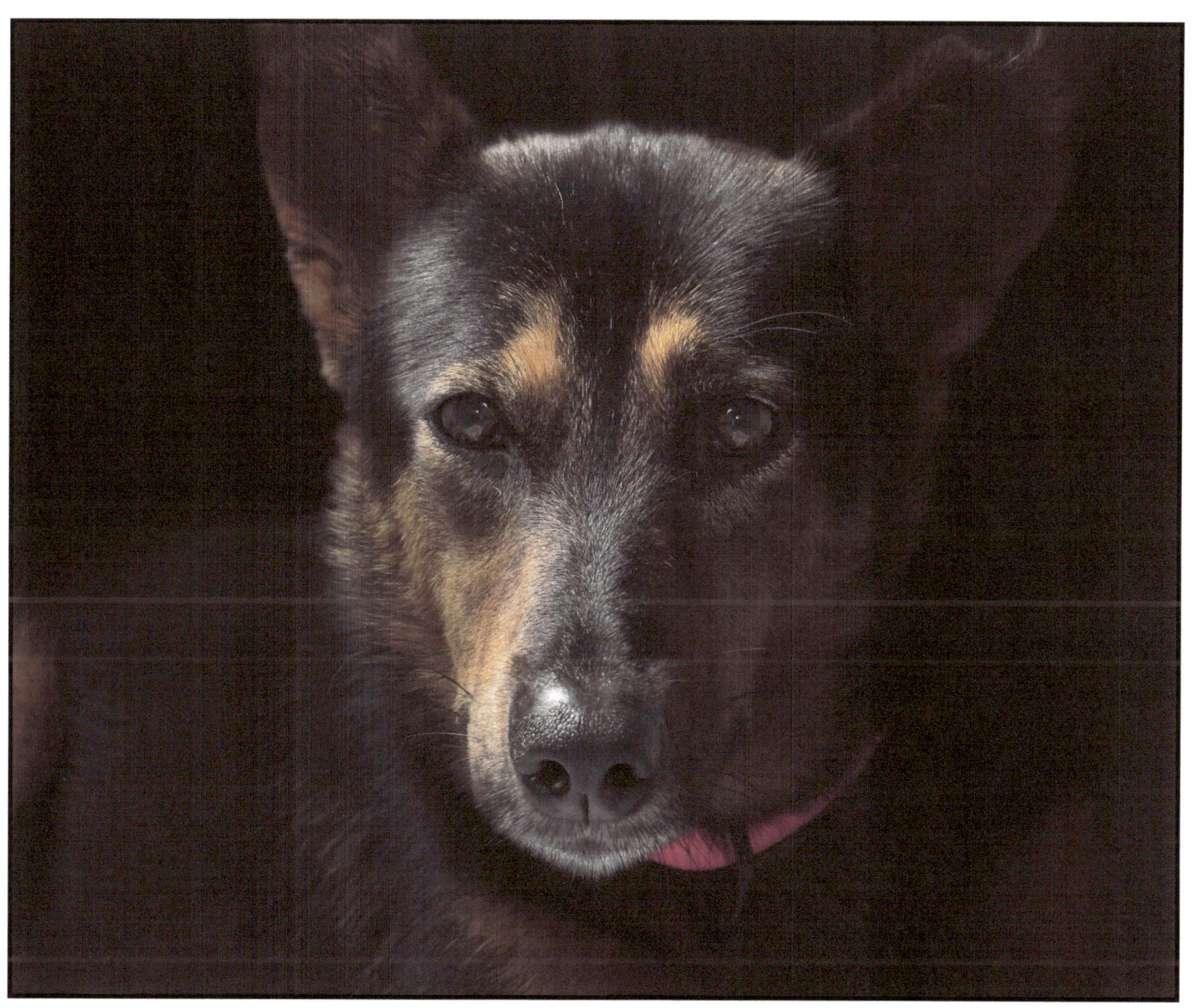

Shina

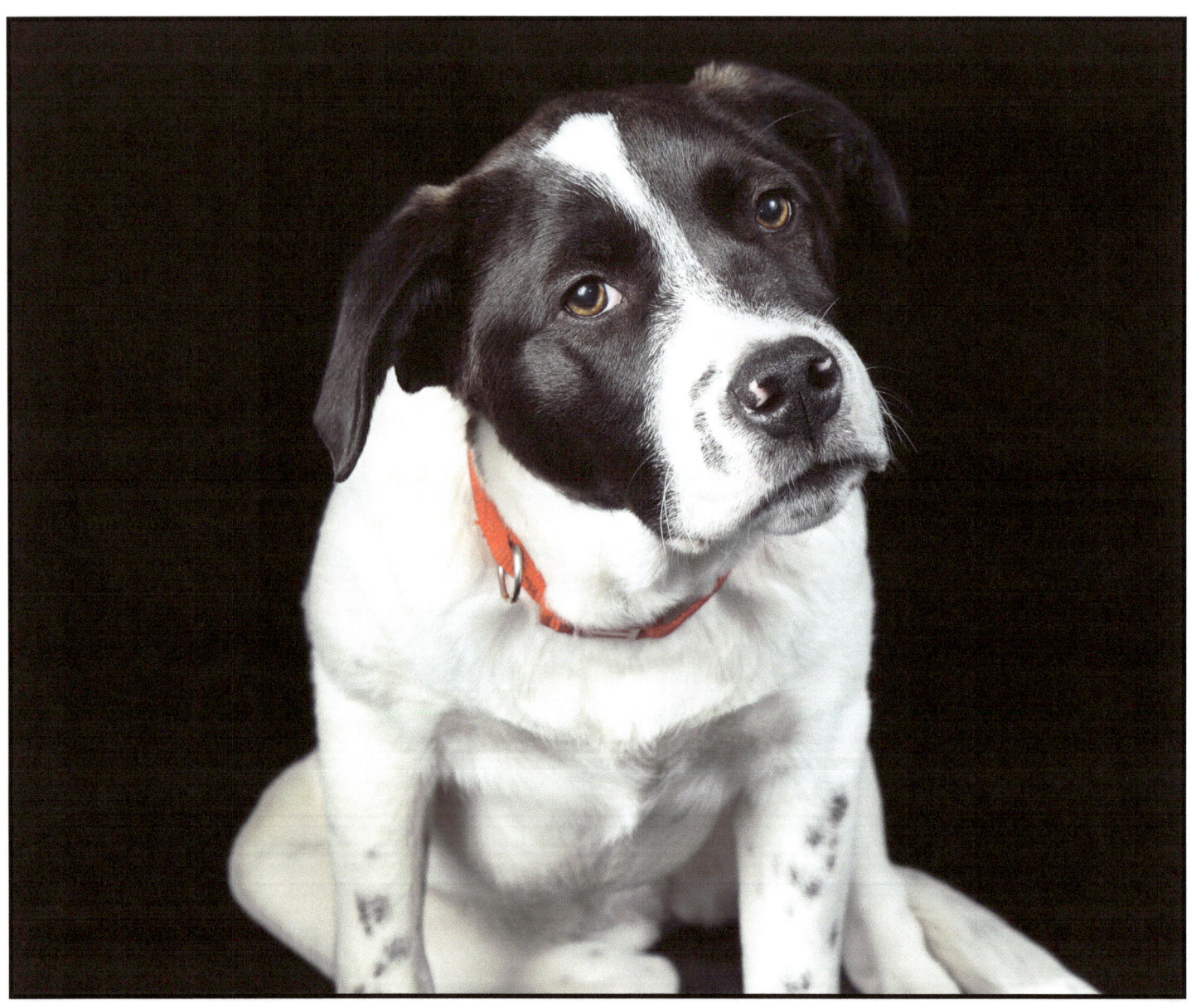

Bella

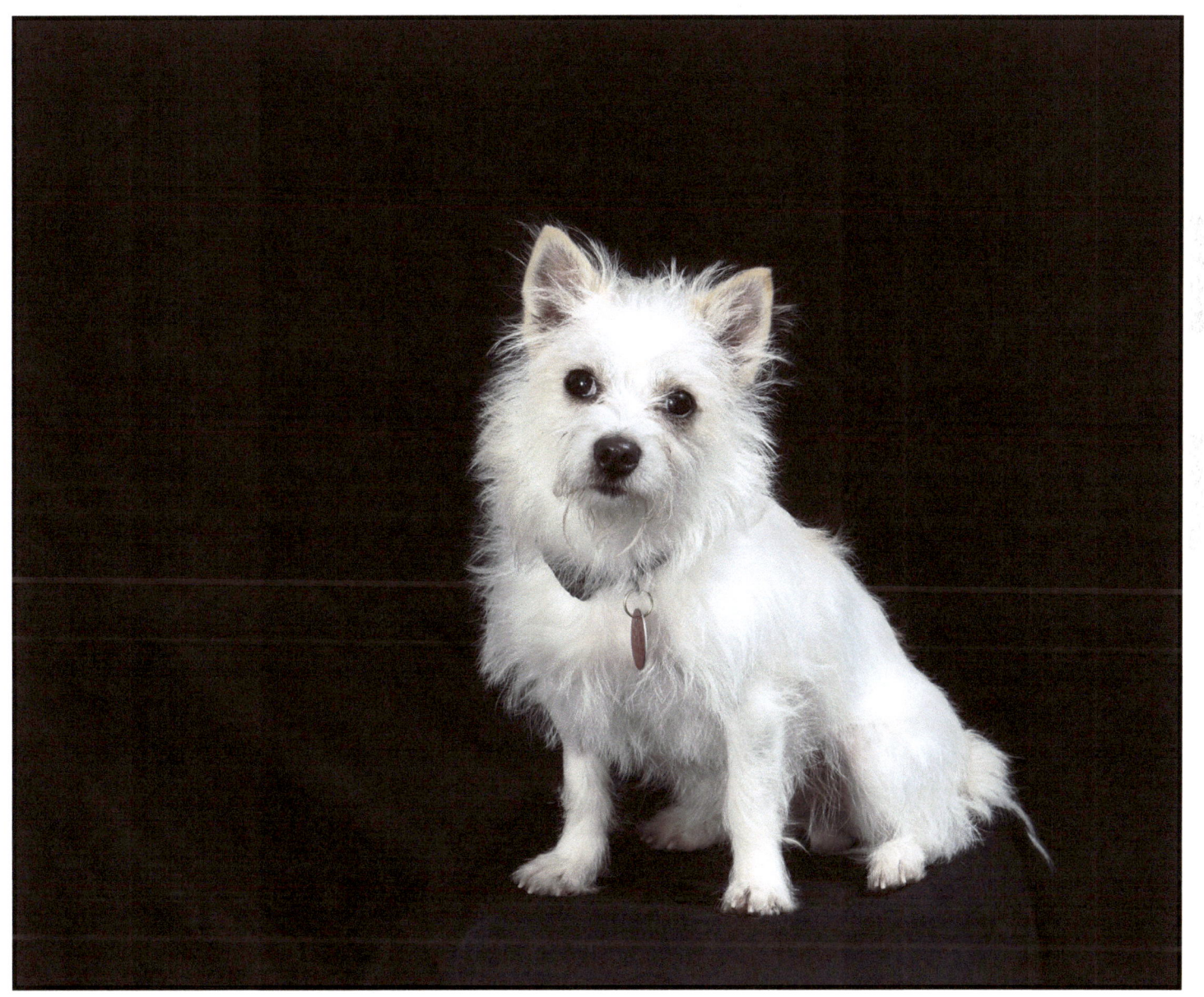

Memphis

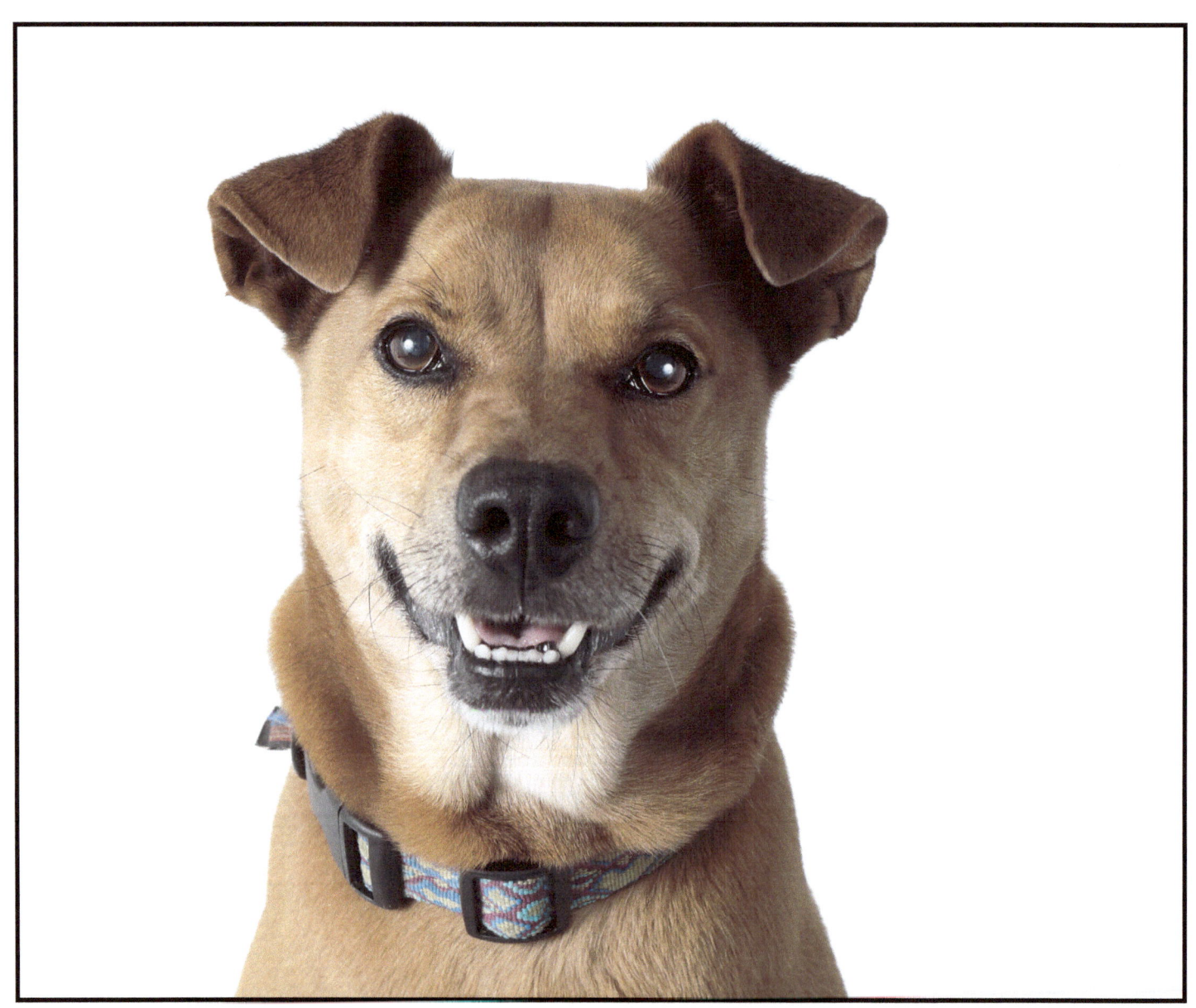

Napolean

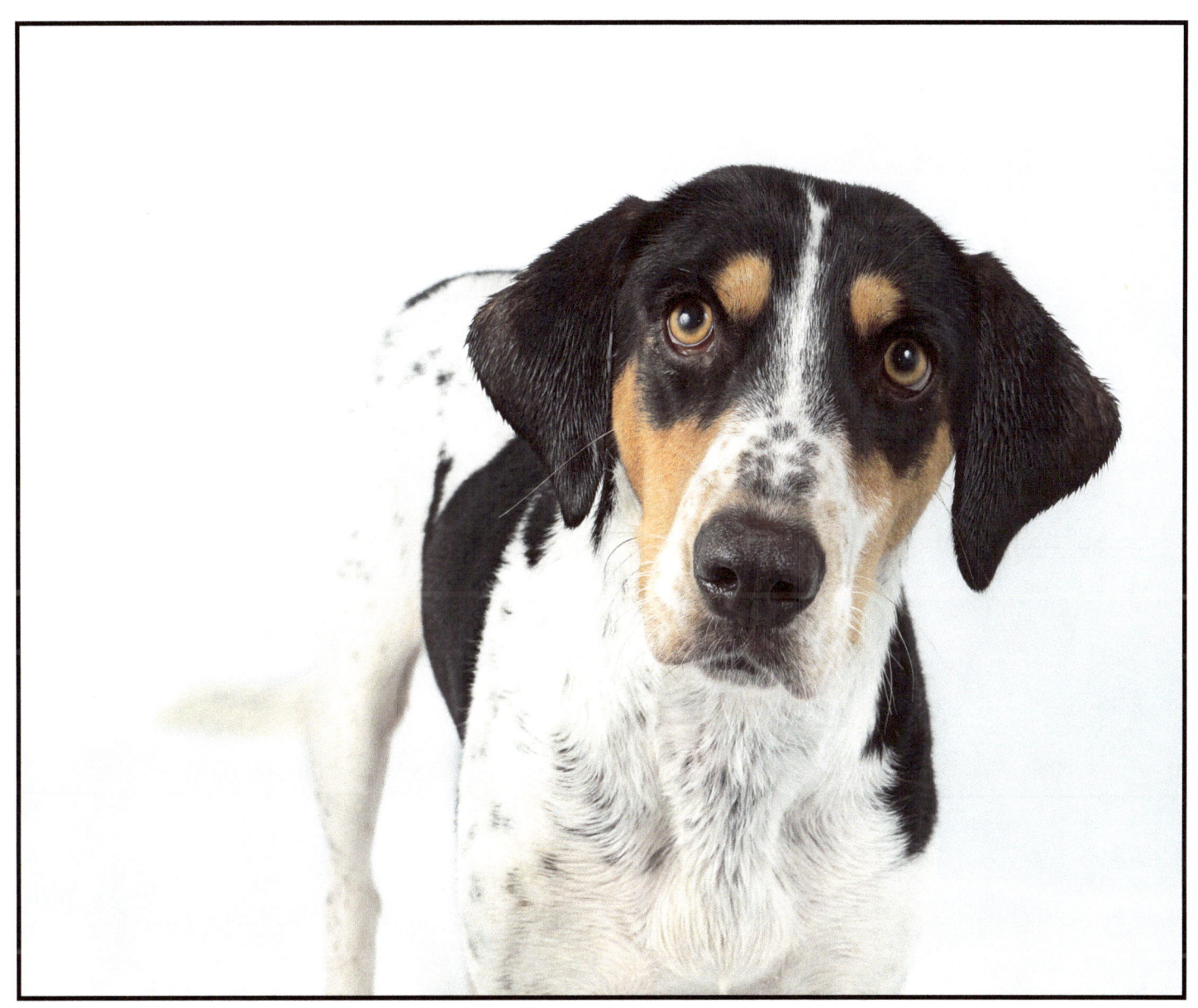

Georgia

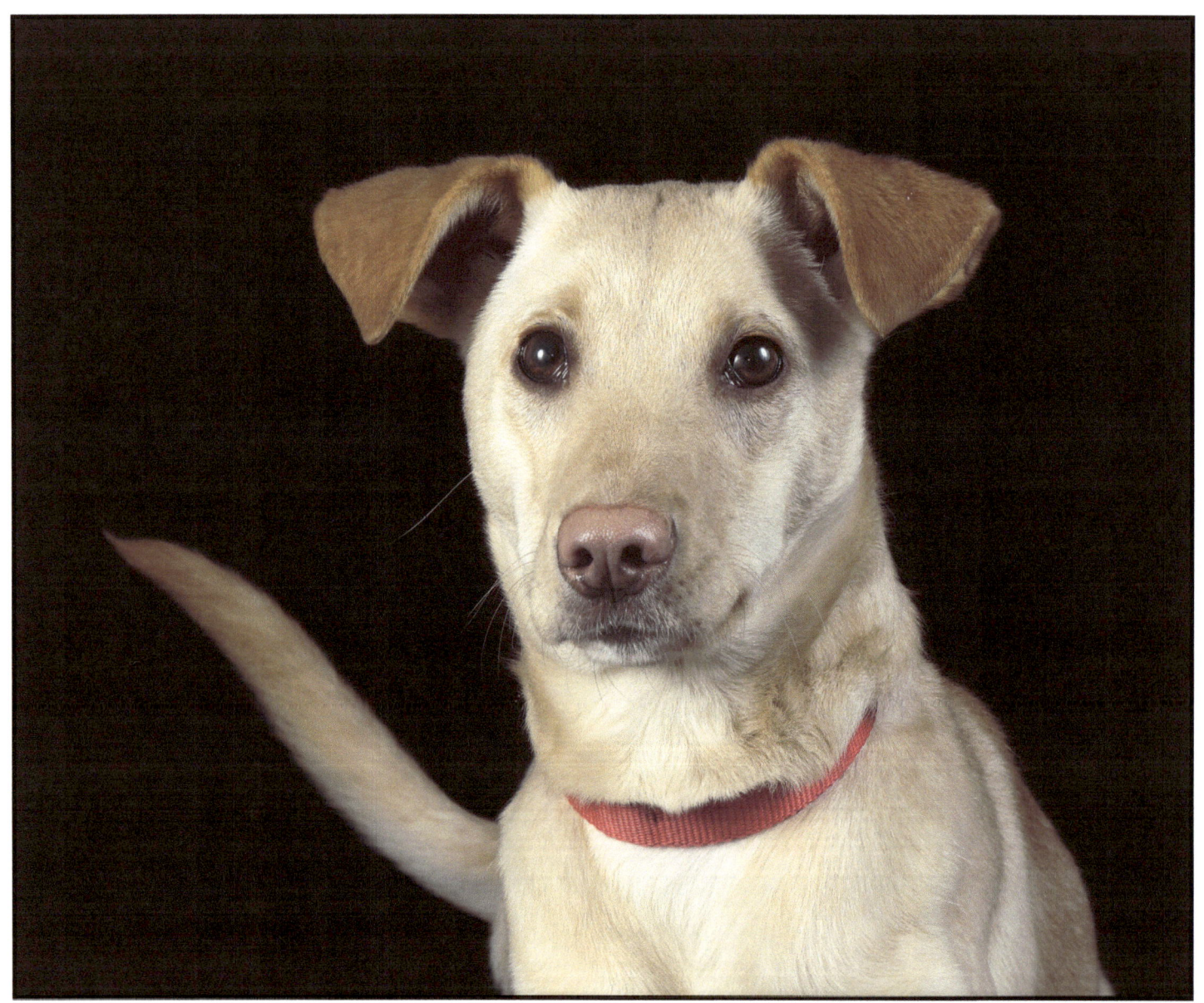

Rainbow

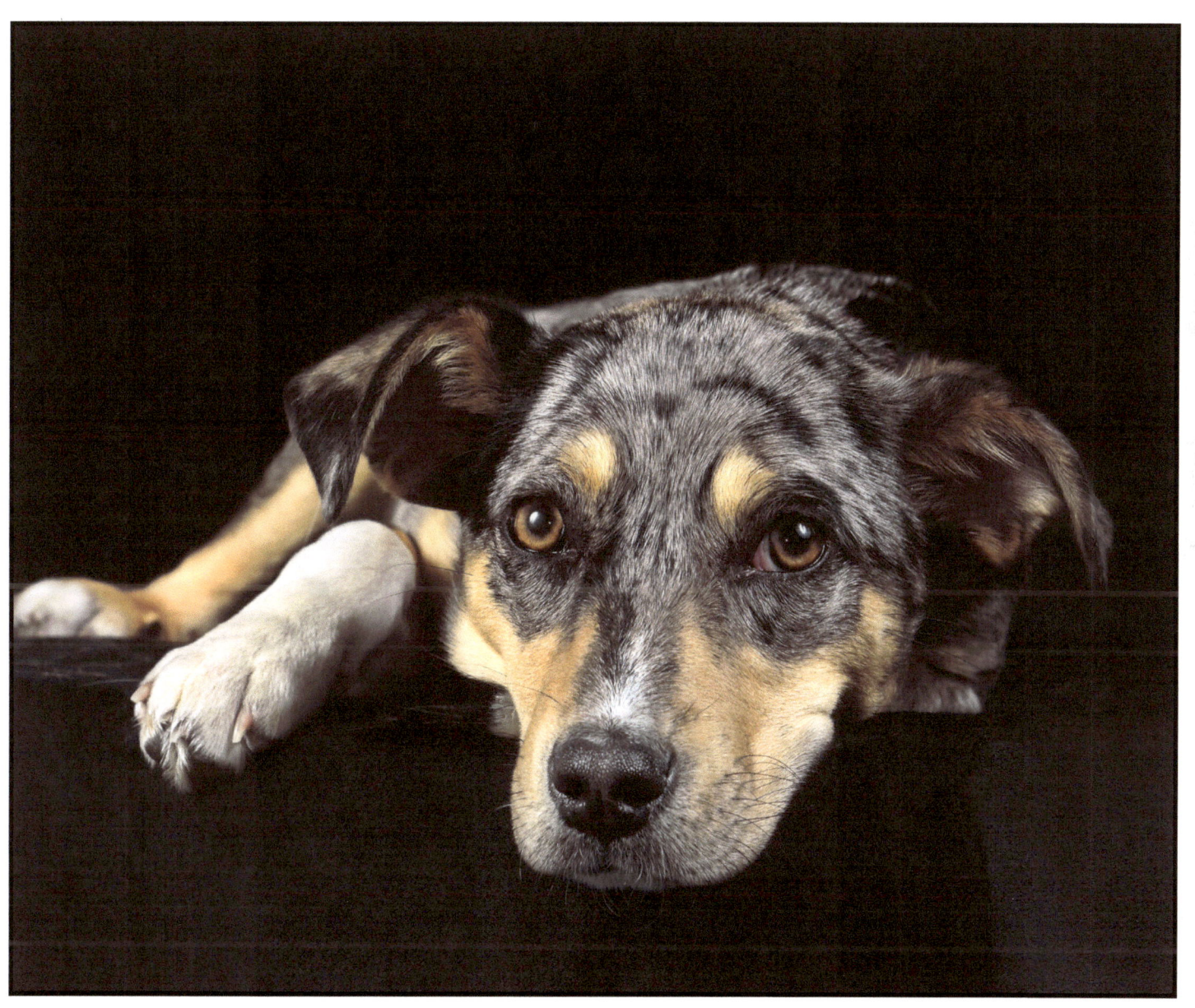

Cameo

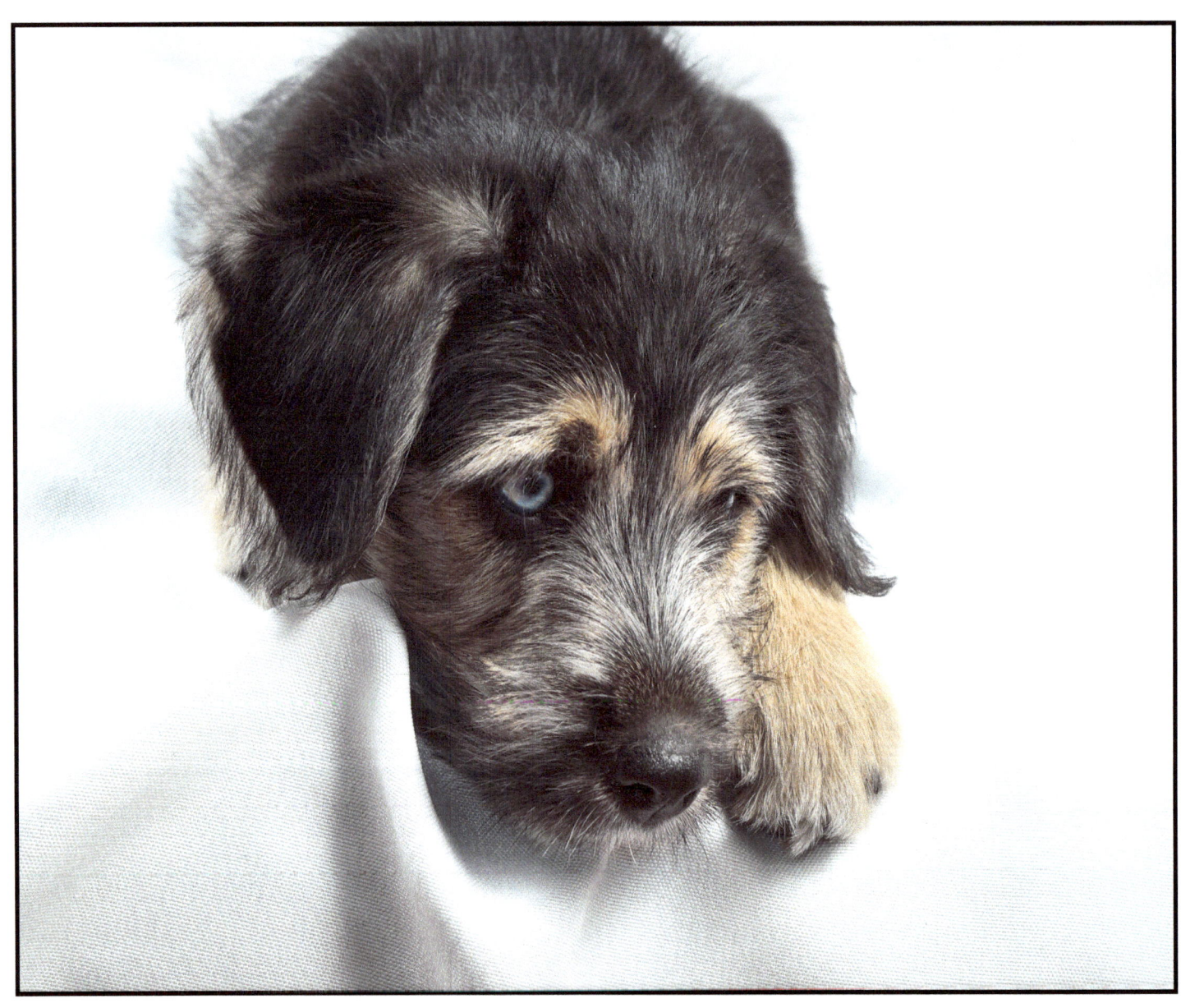

Roxie

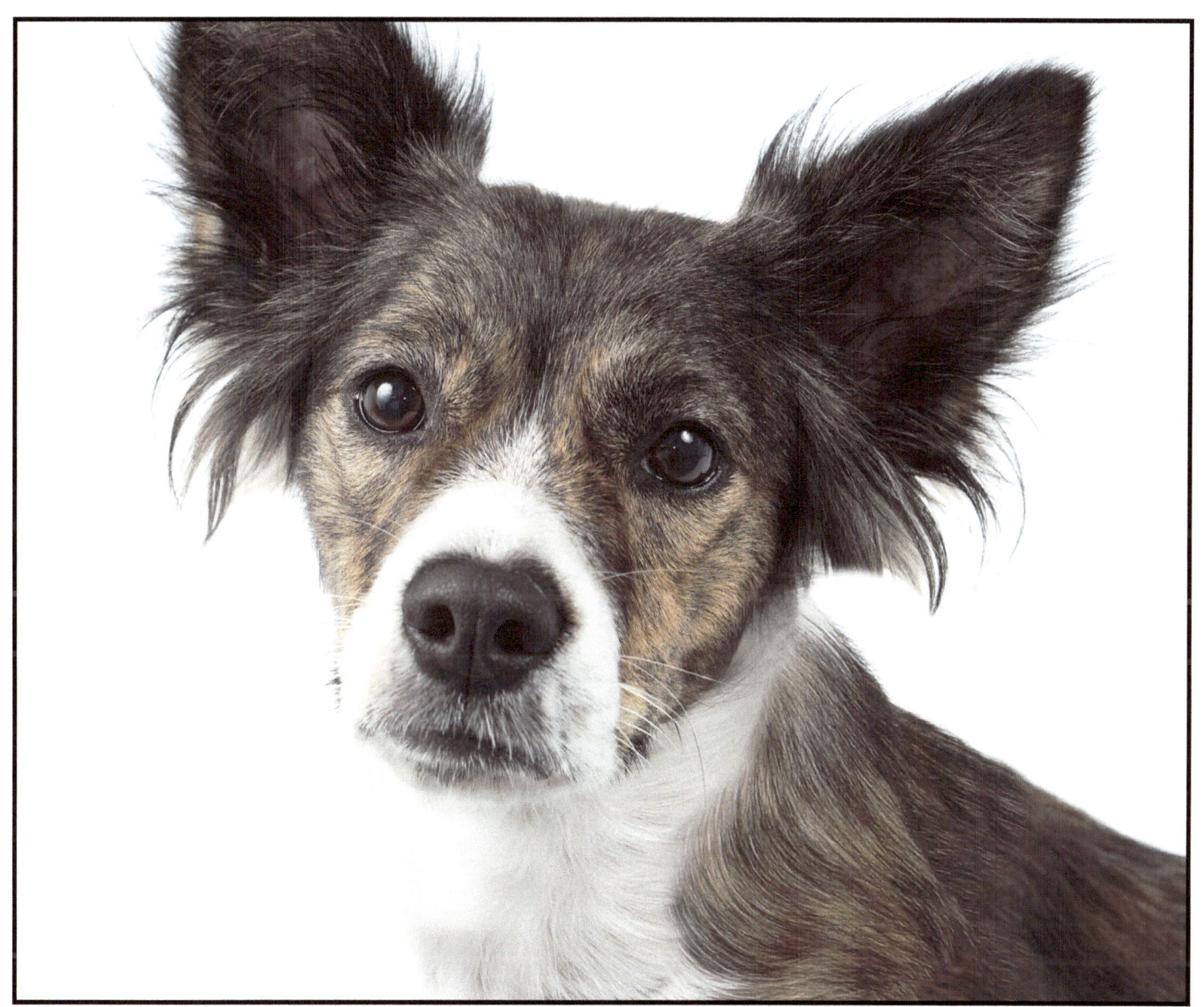

Dixie

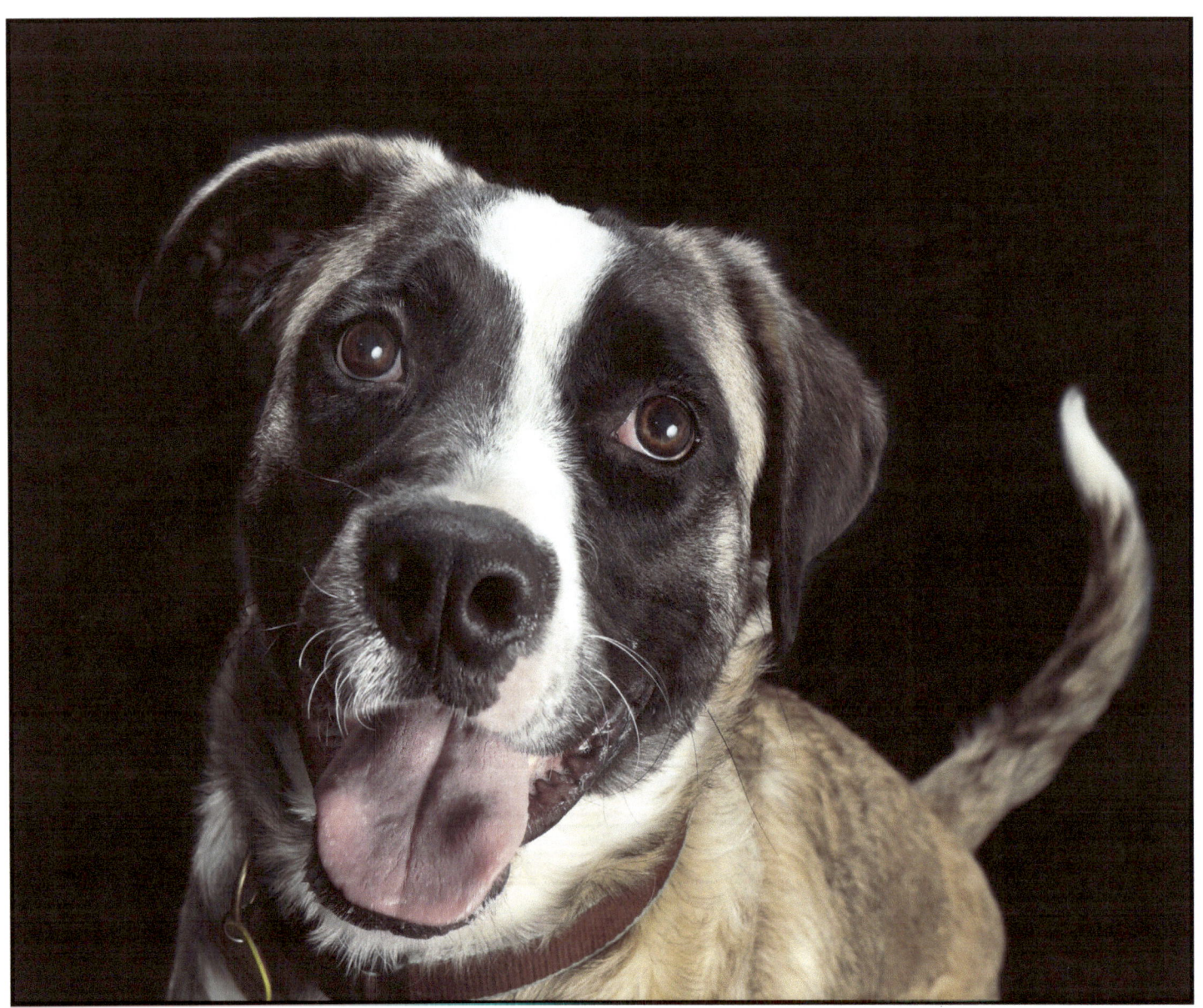

Barney

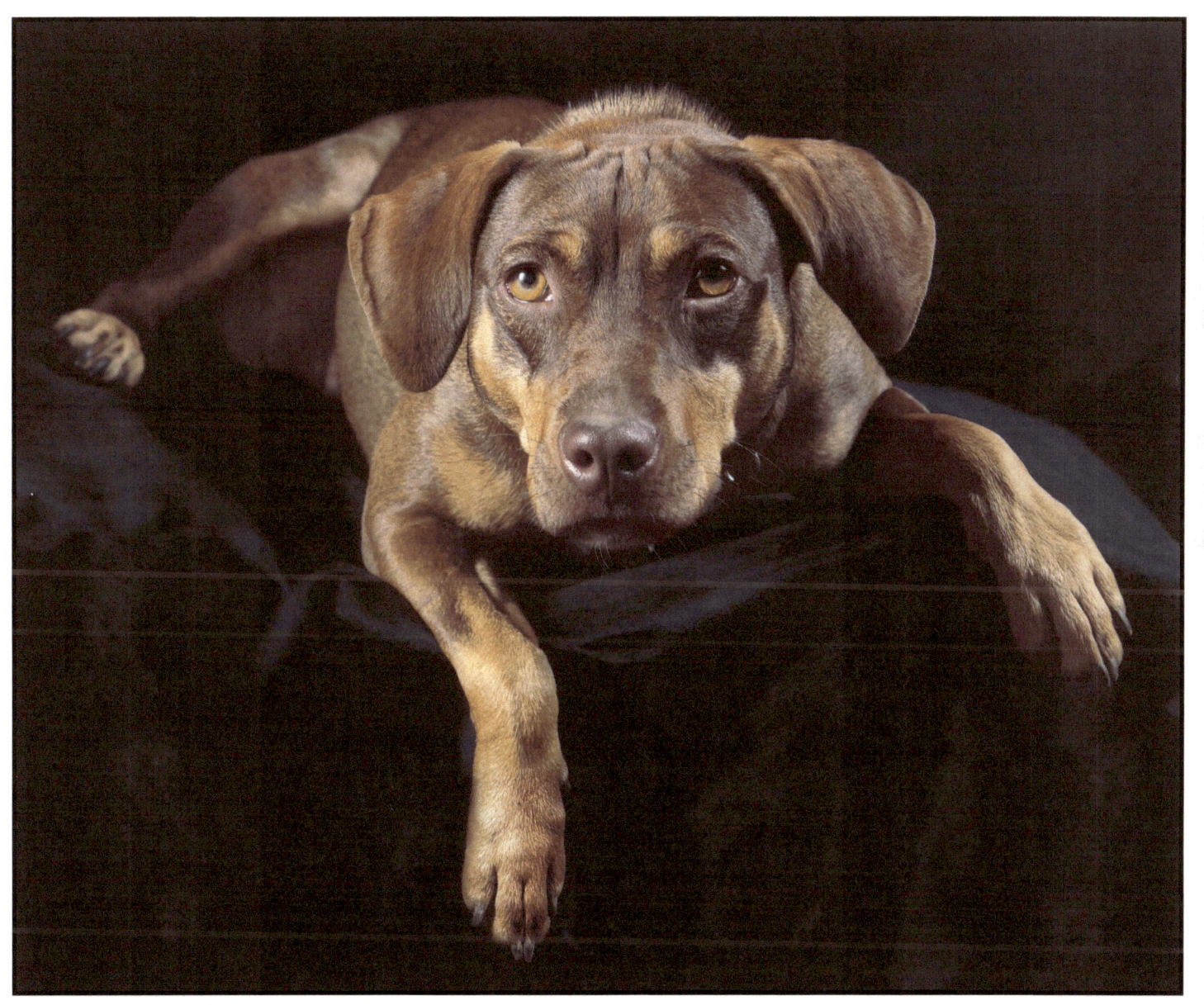

Reeses

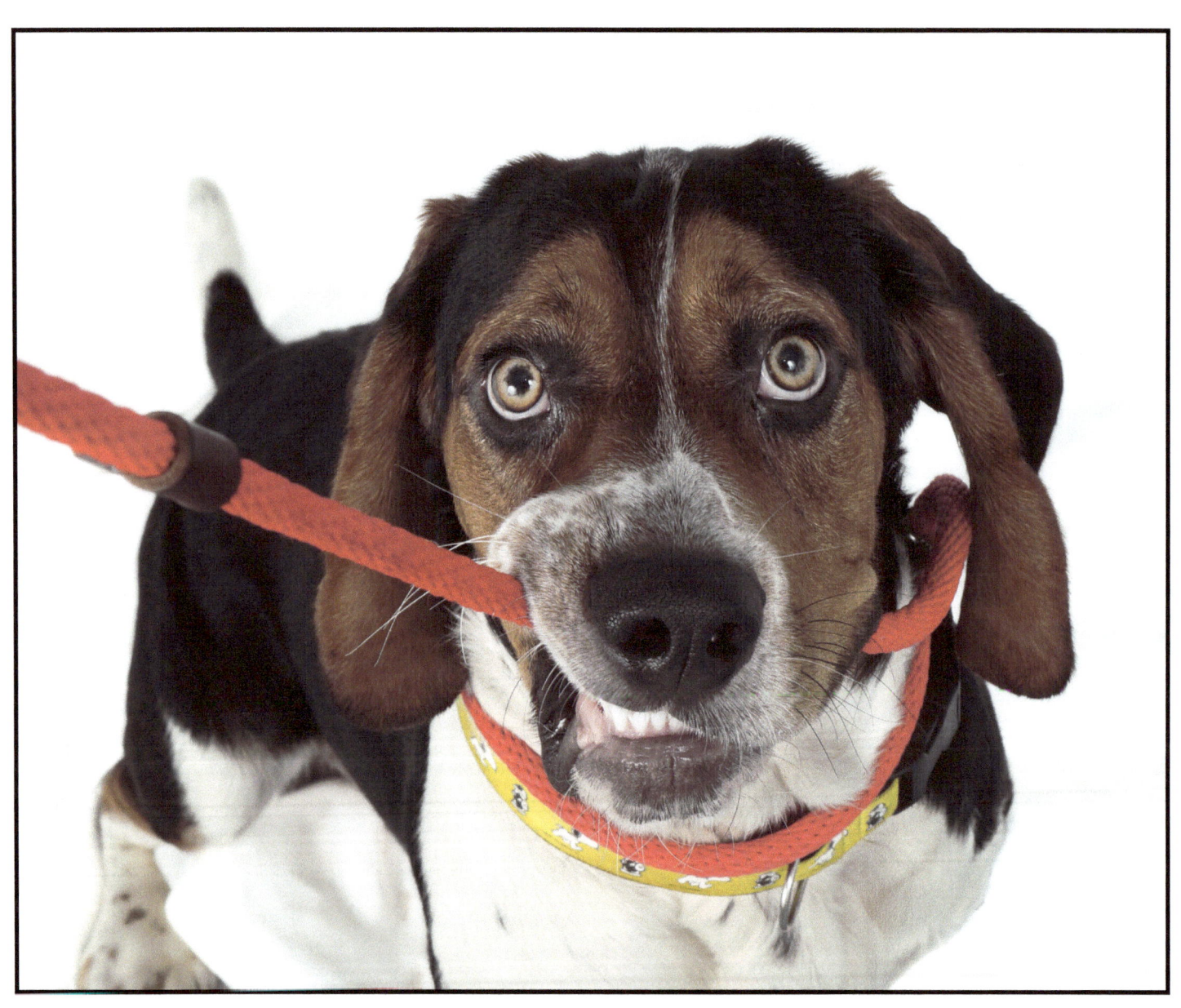

Smoochie

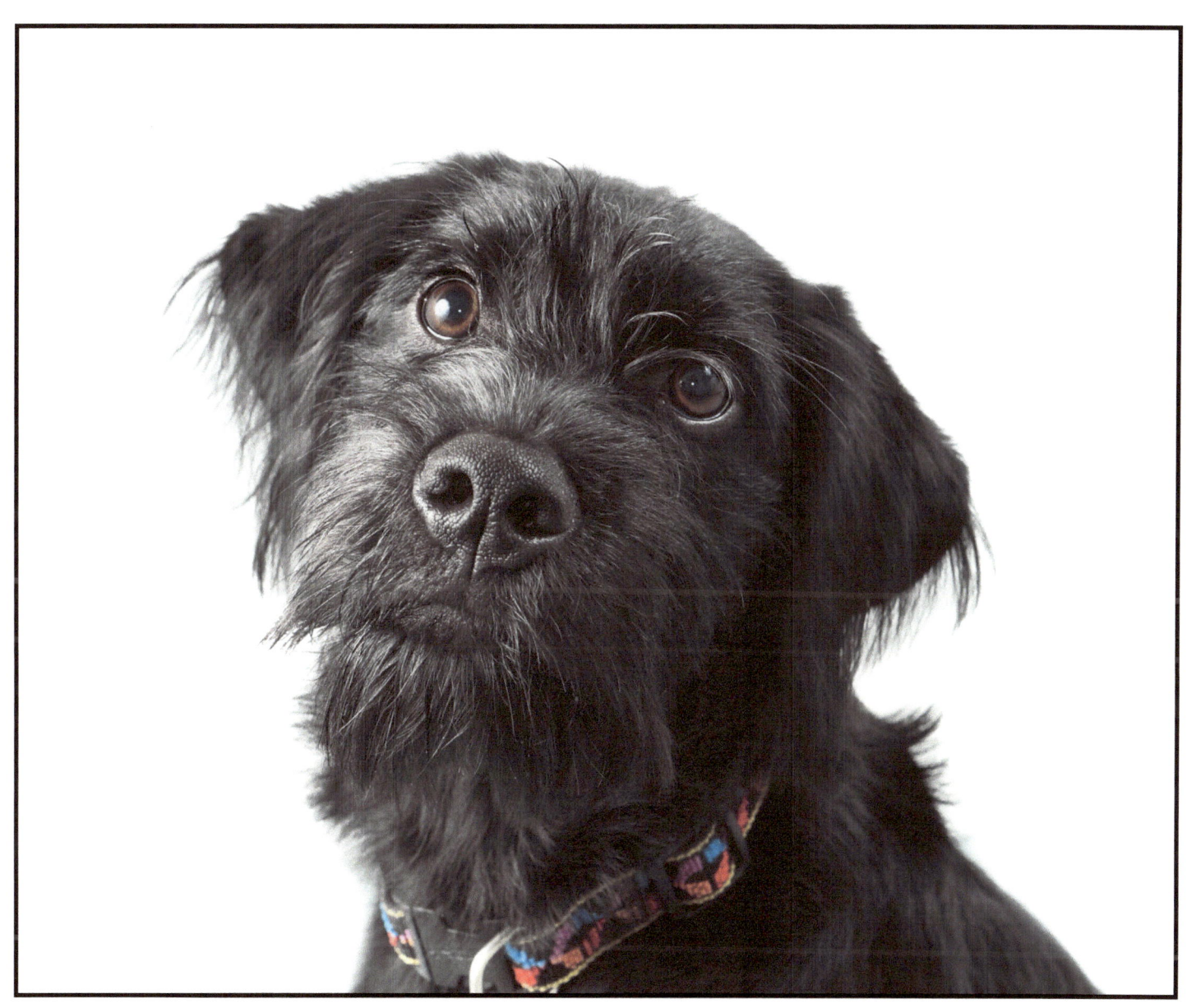

Presley

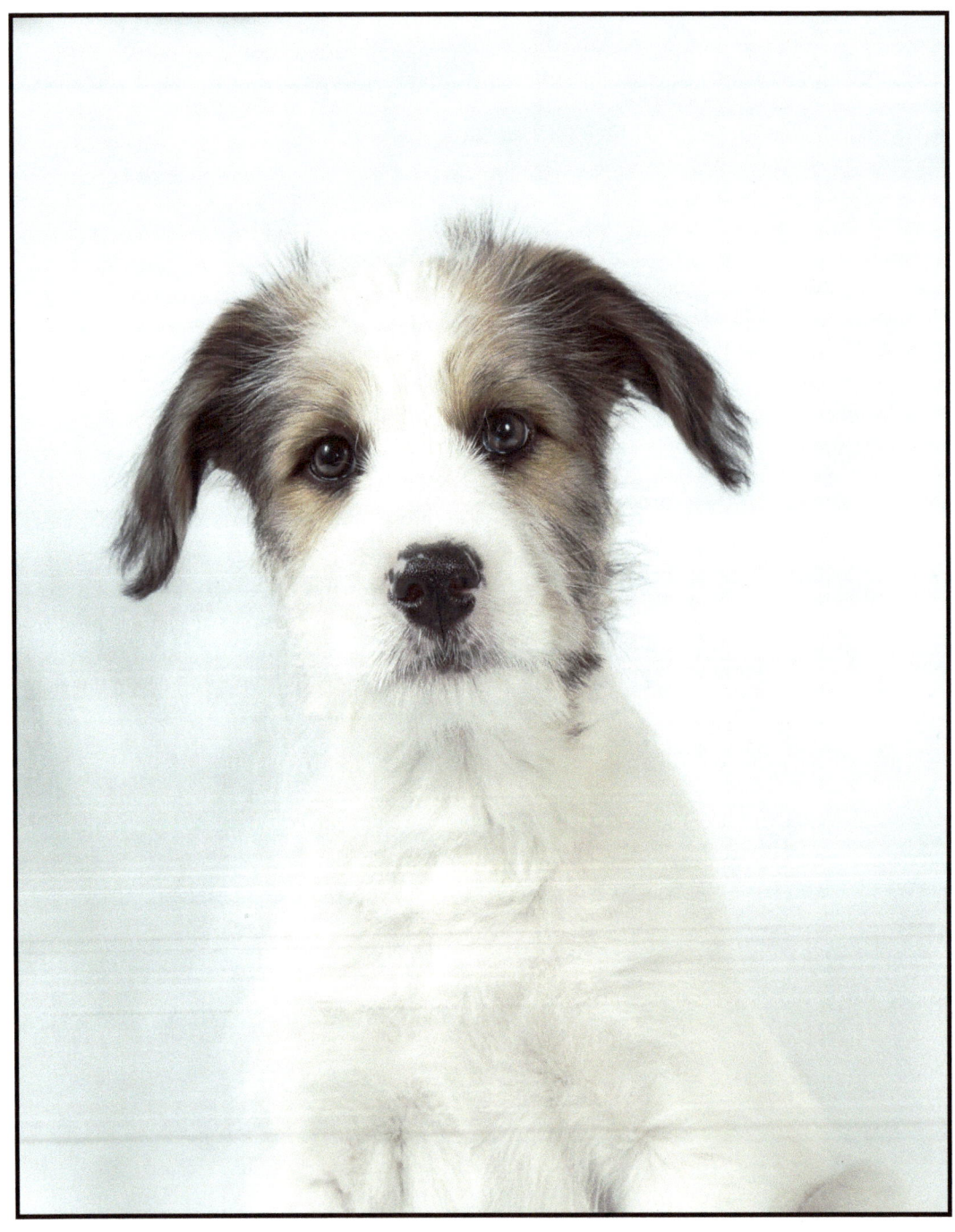

Rocket

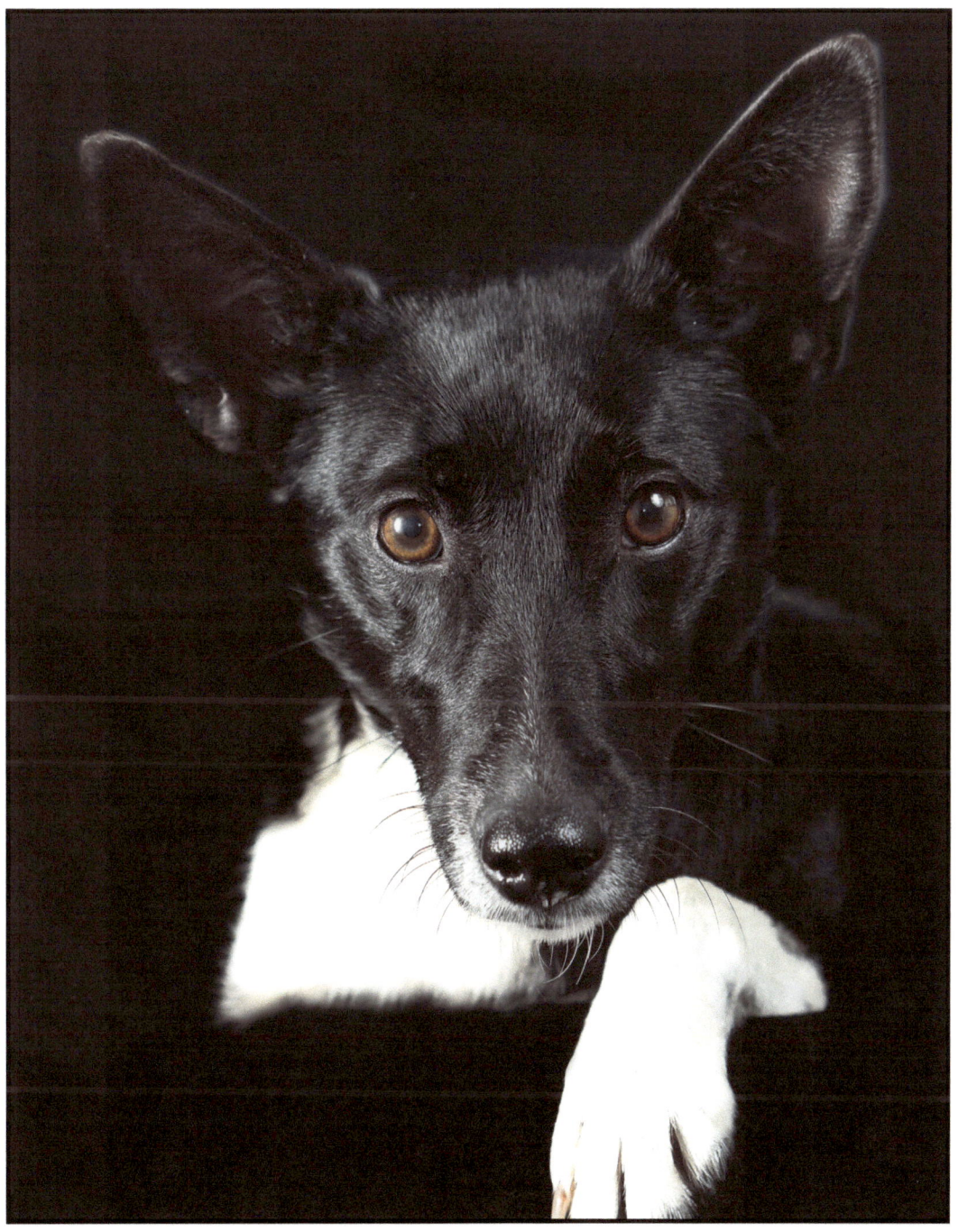

Tamera

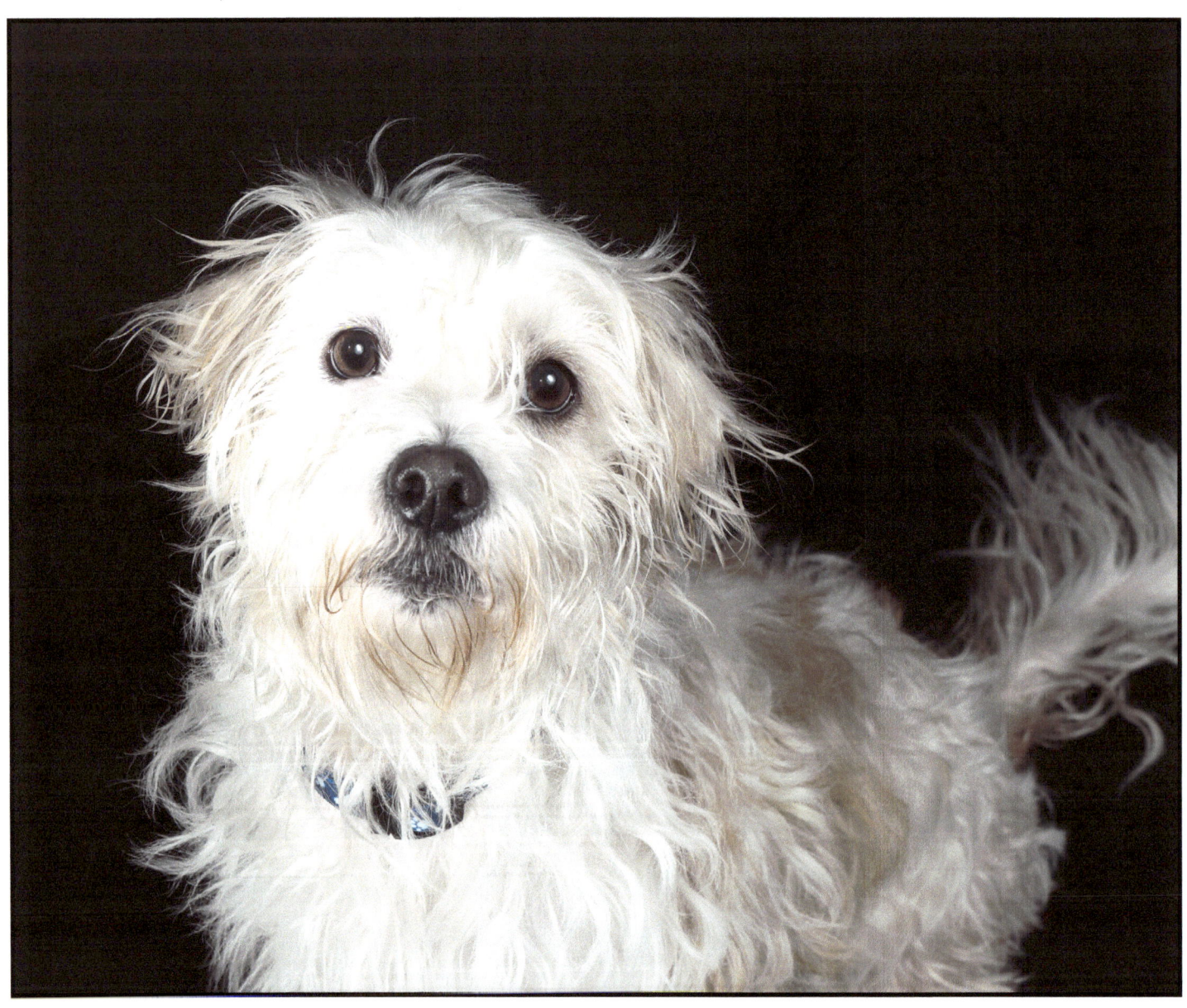

Jolly

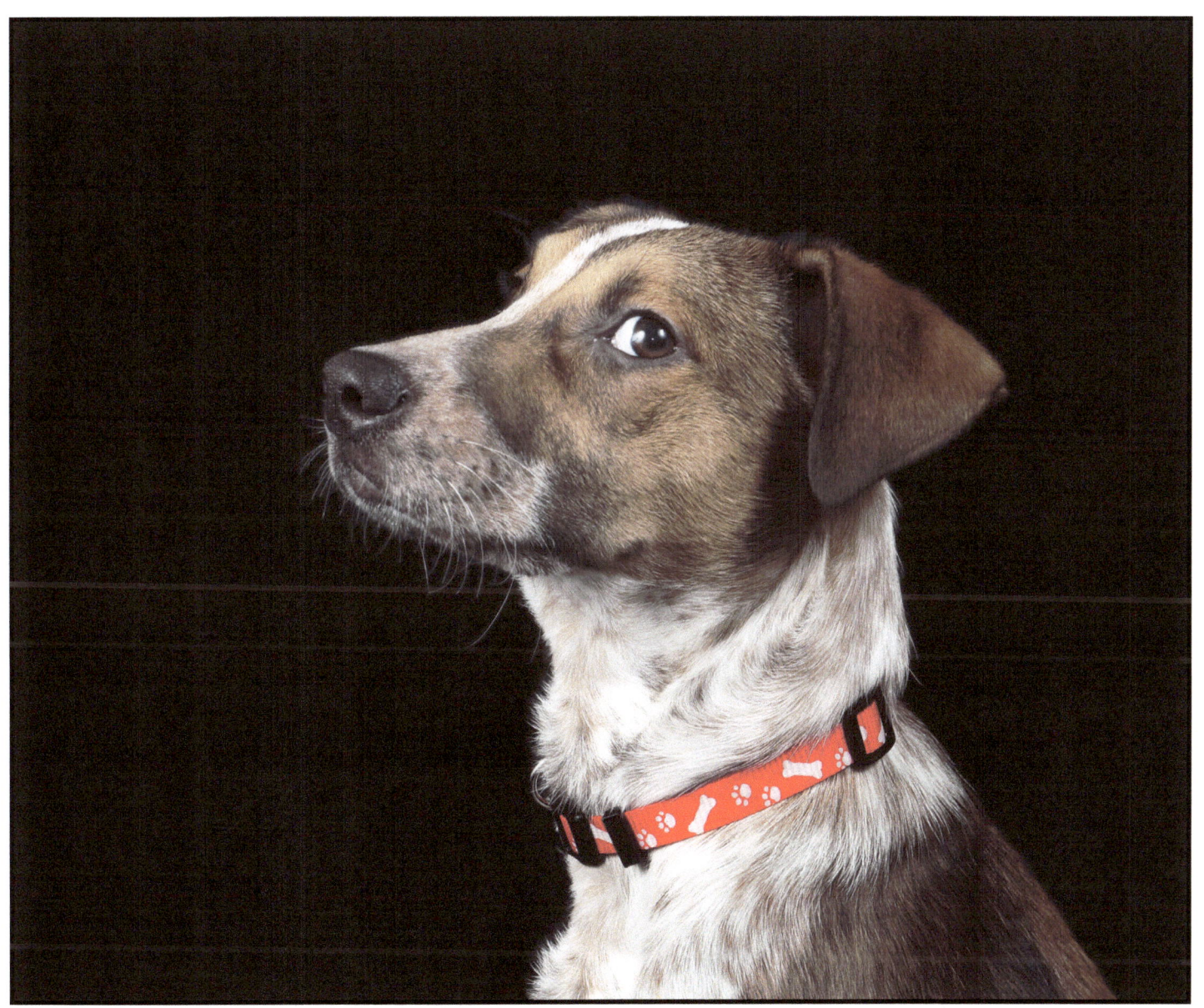

Cinnamon

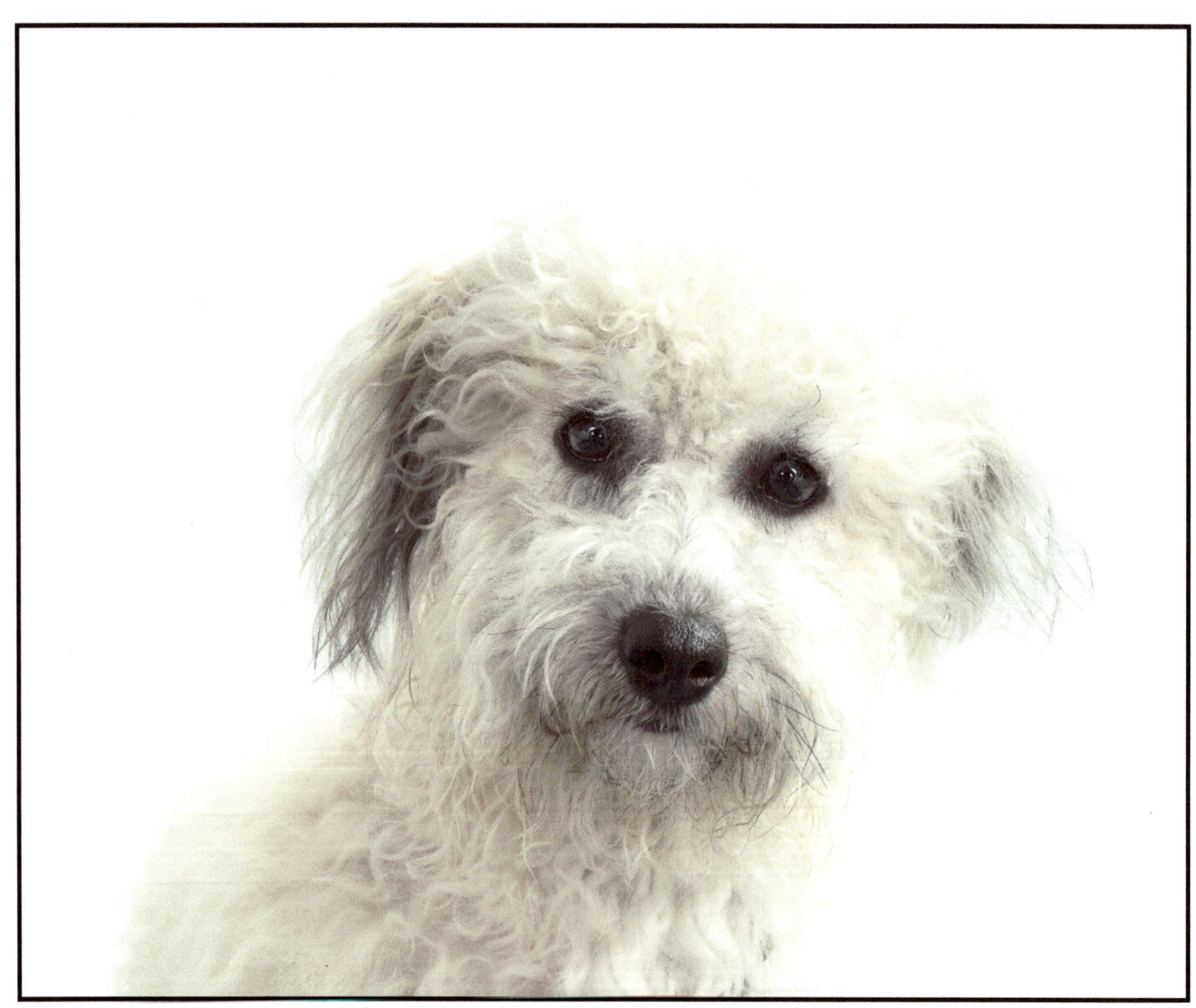

Kiki

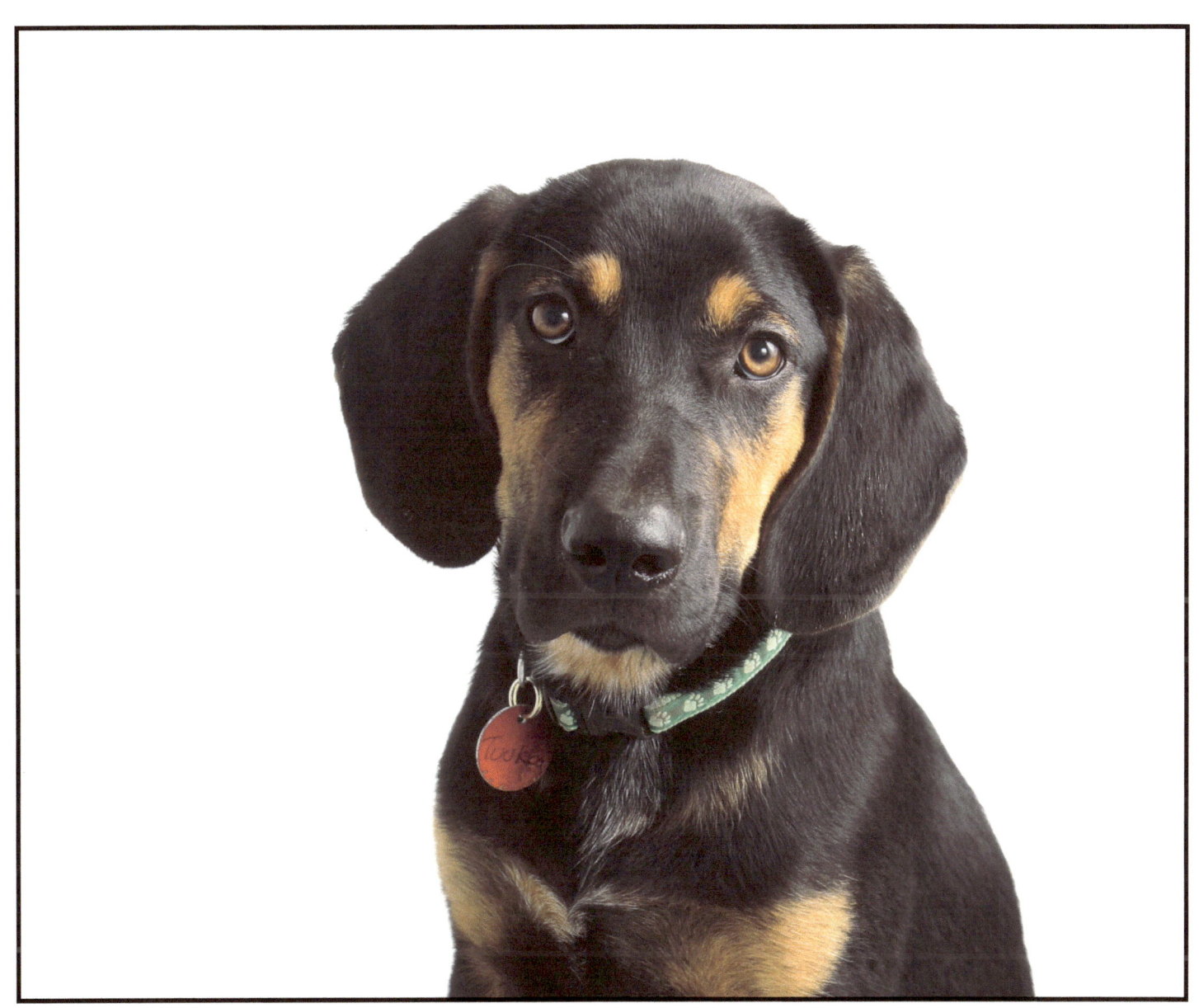

Tuuka

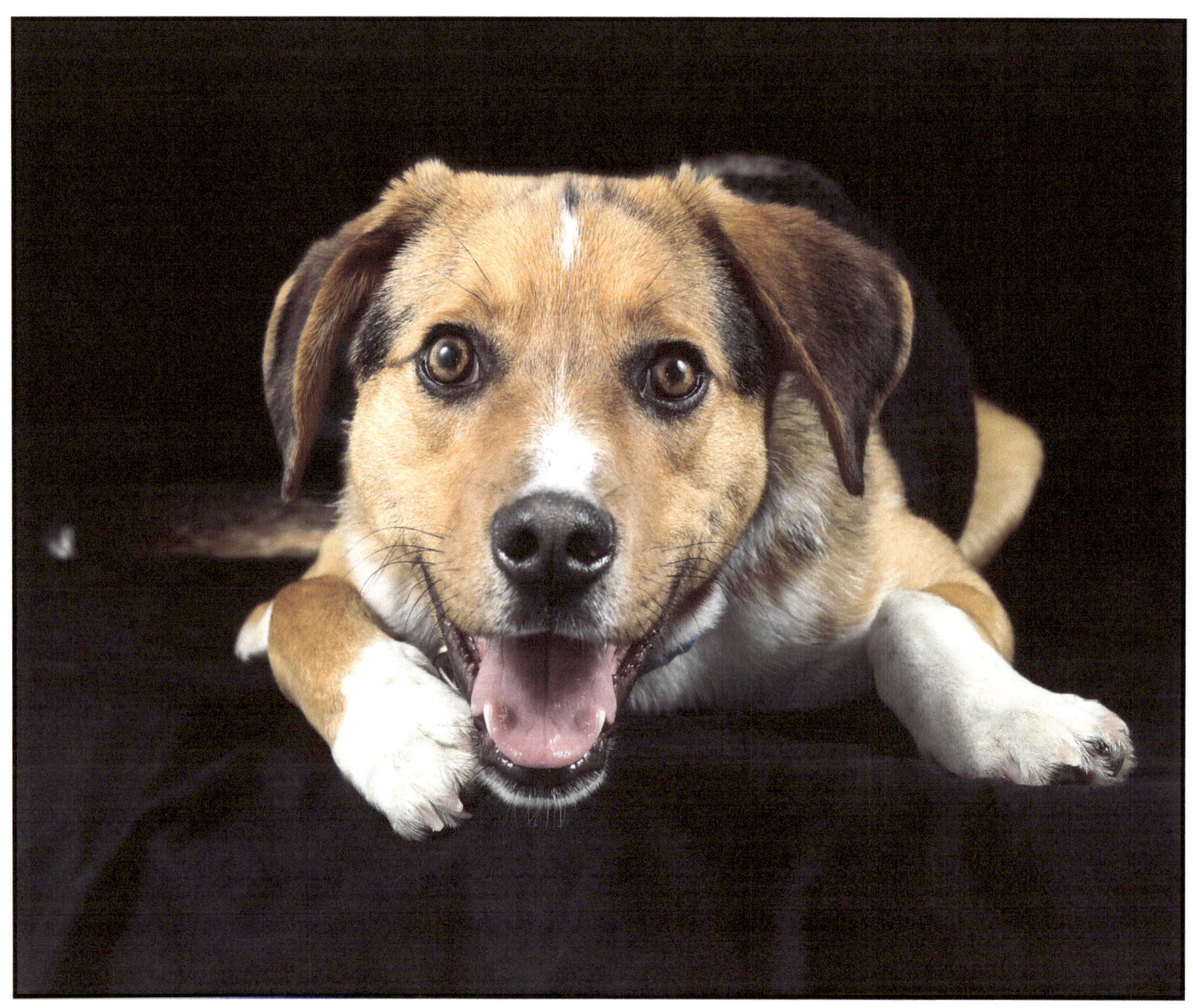

Kula

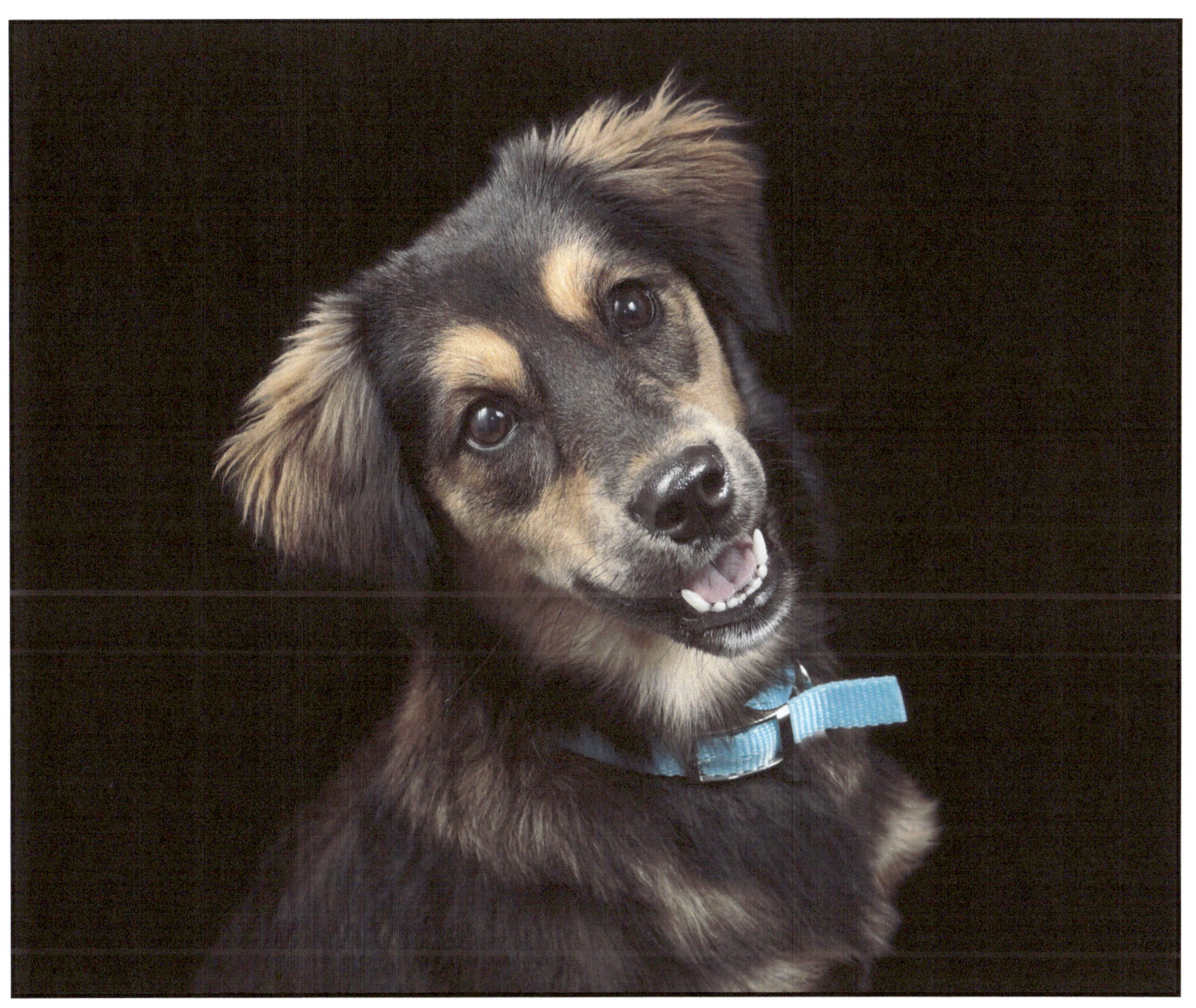

Mulberry

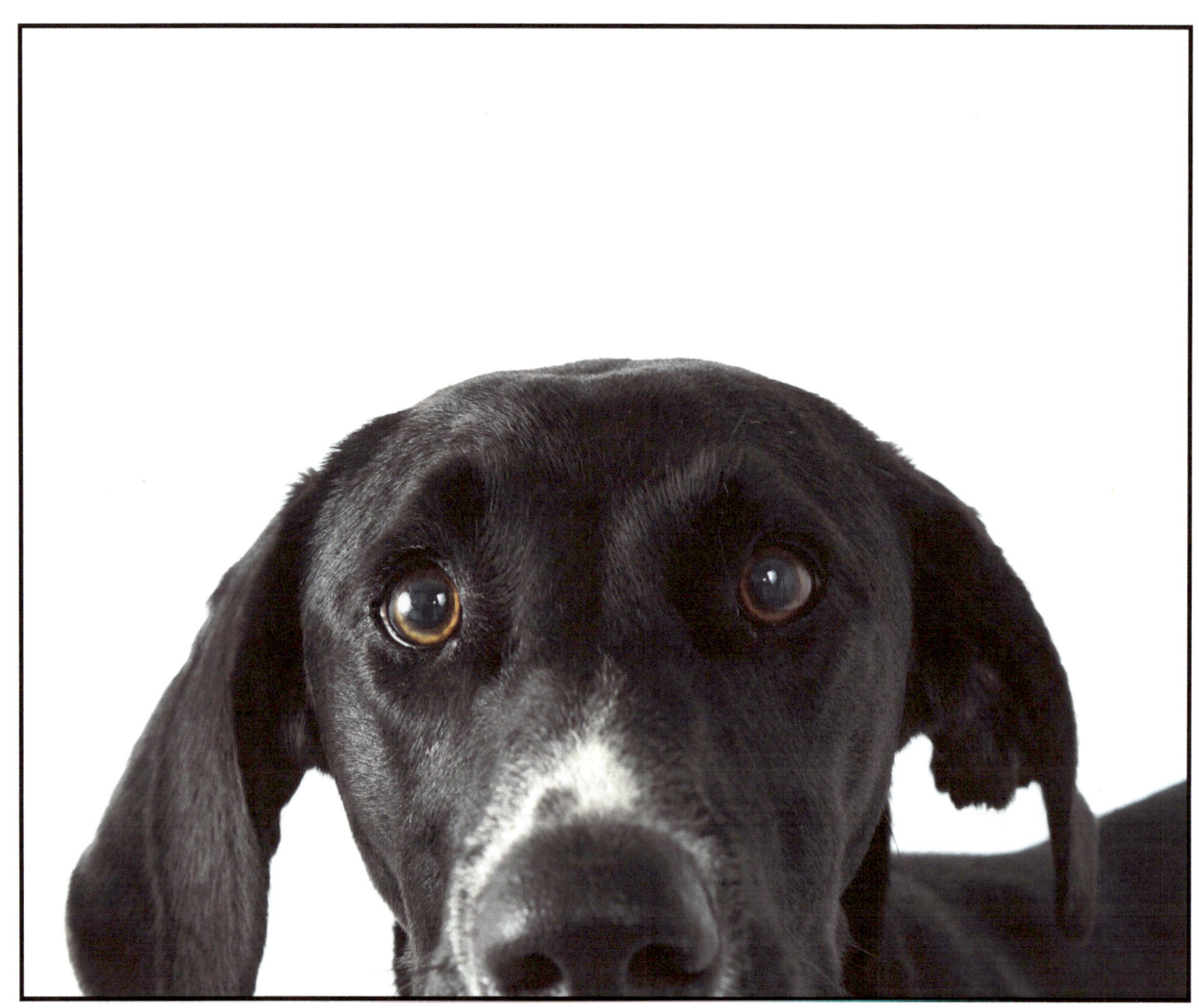

Kulia

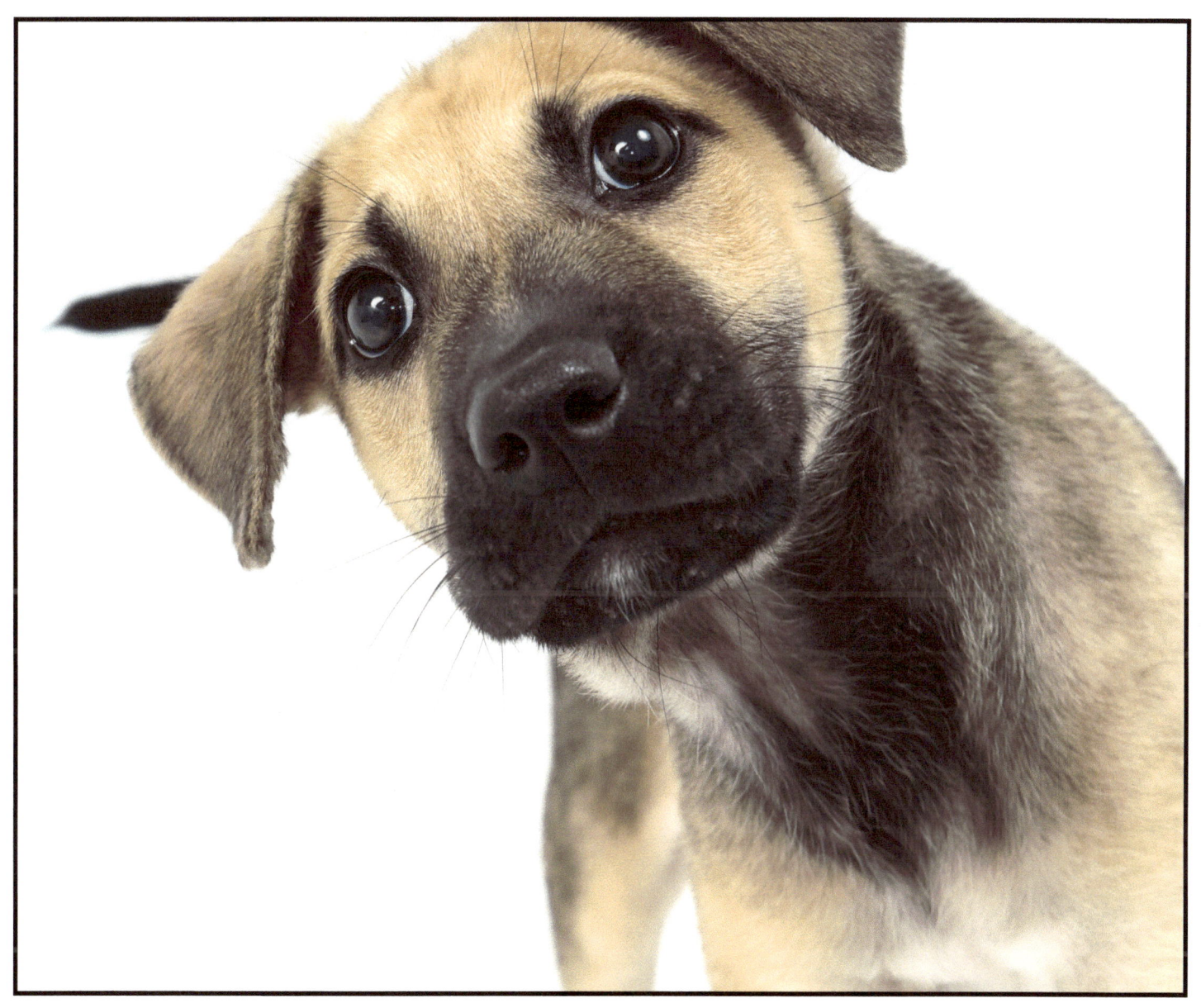

Kellogs

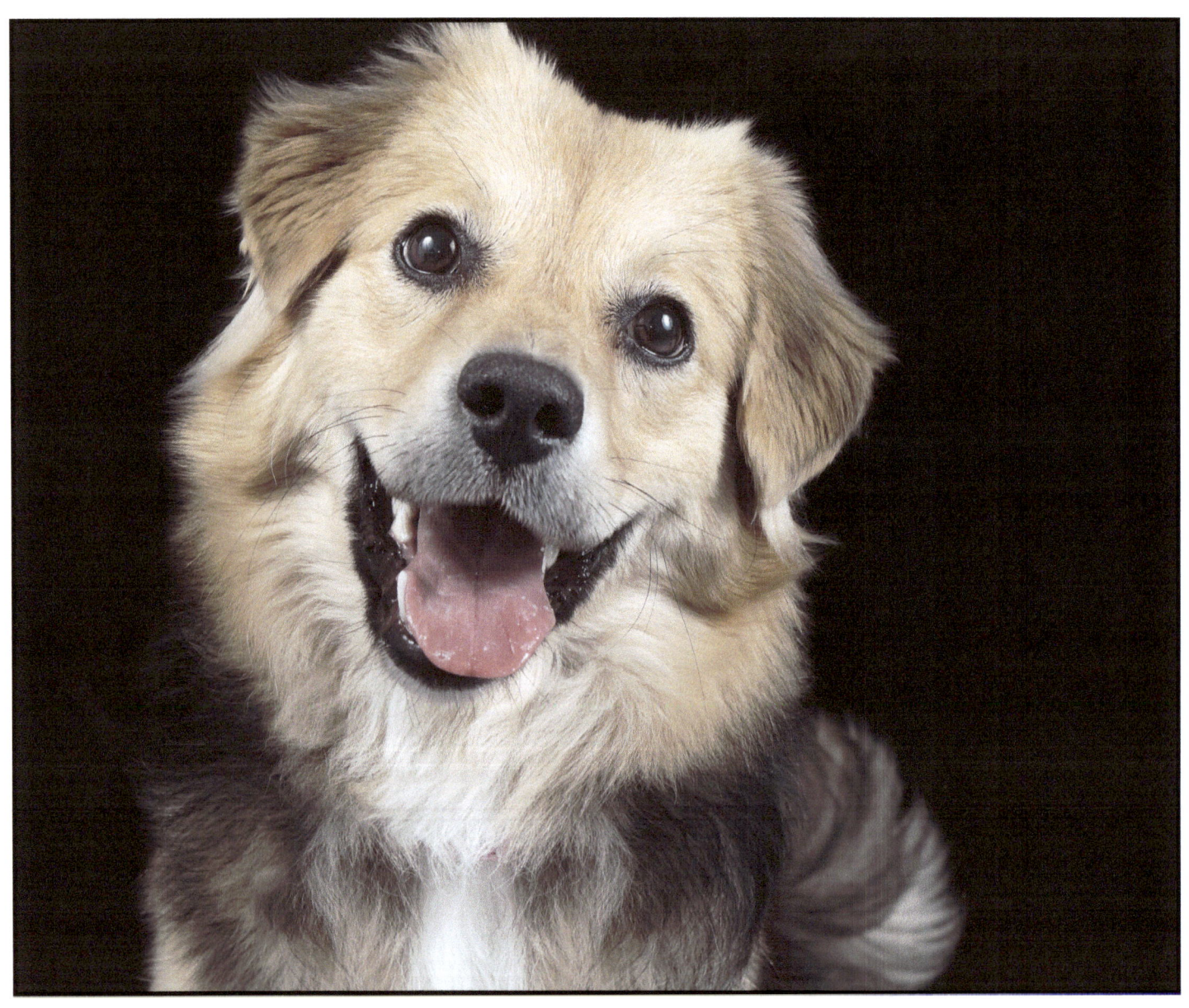

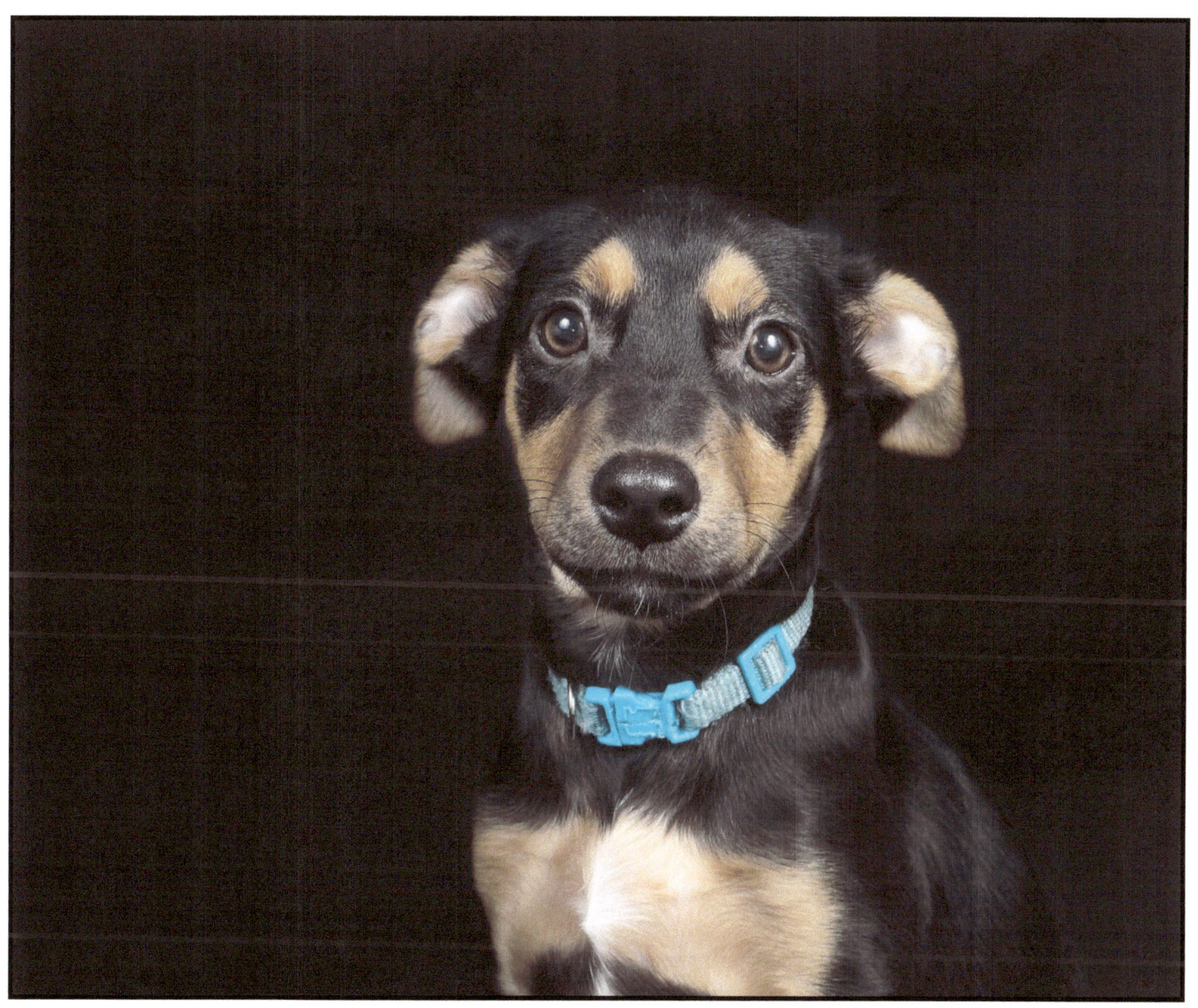

Zephyr

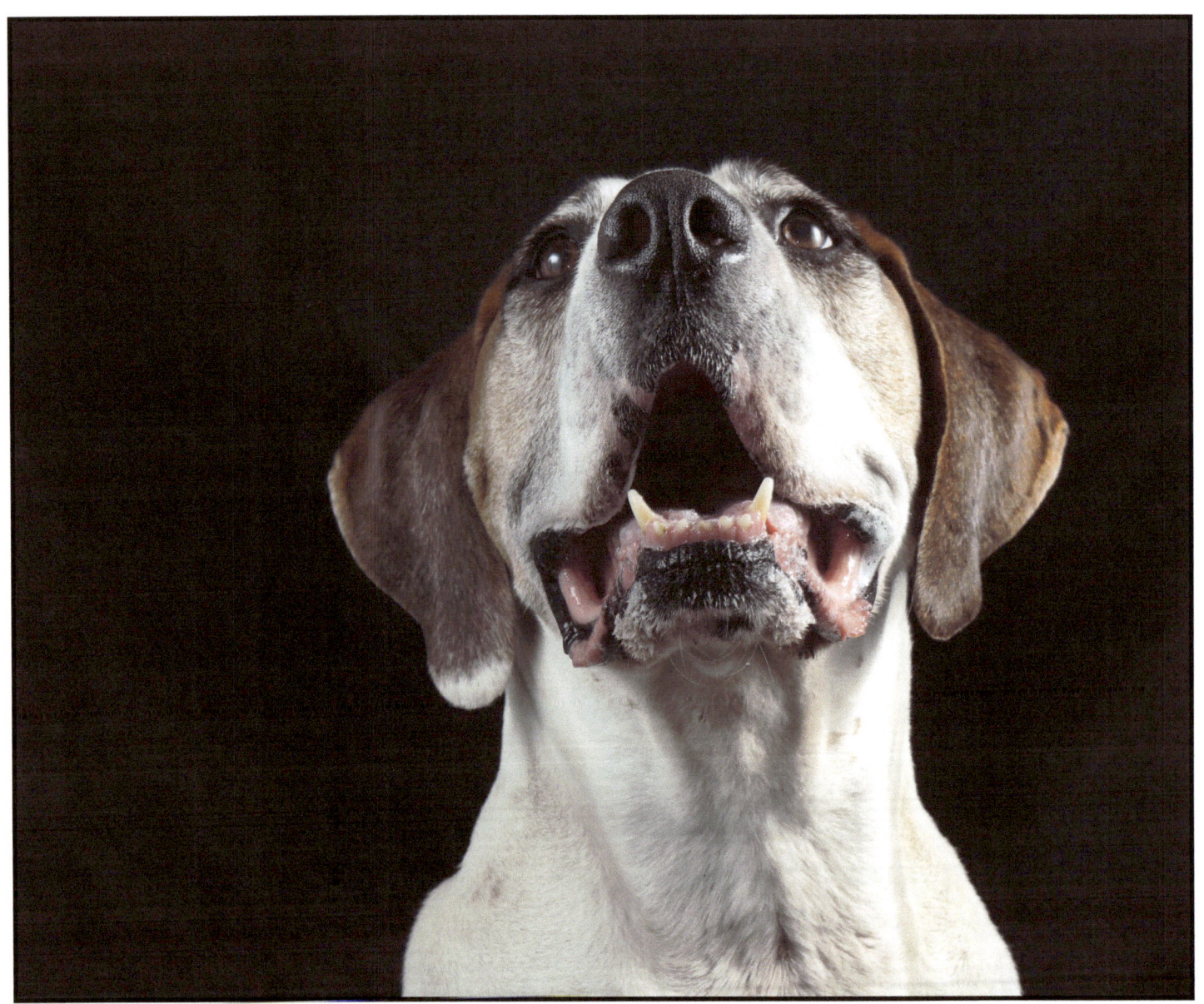

Otis

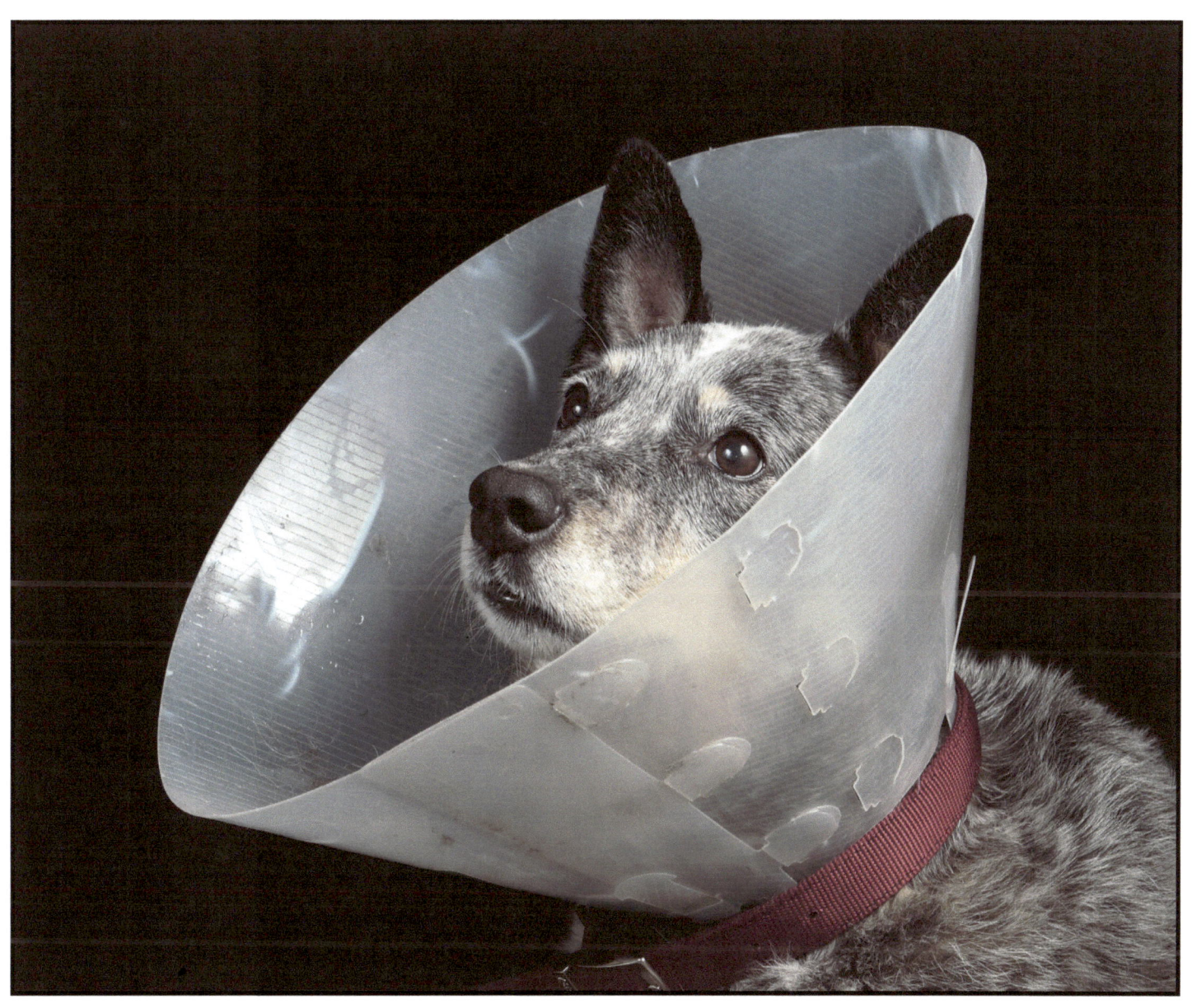

Boca

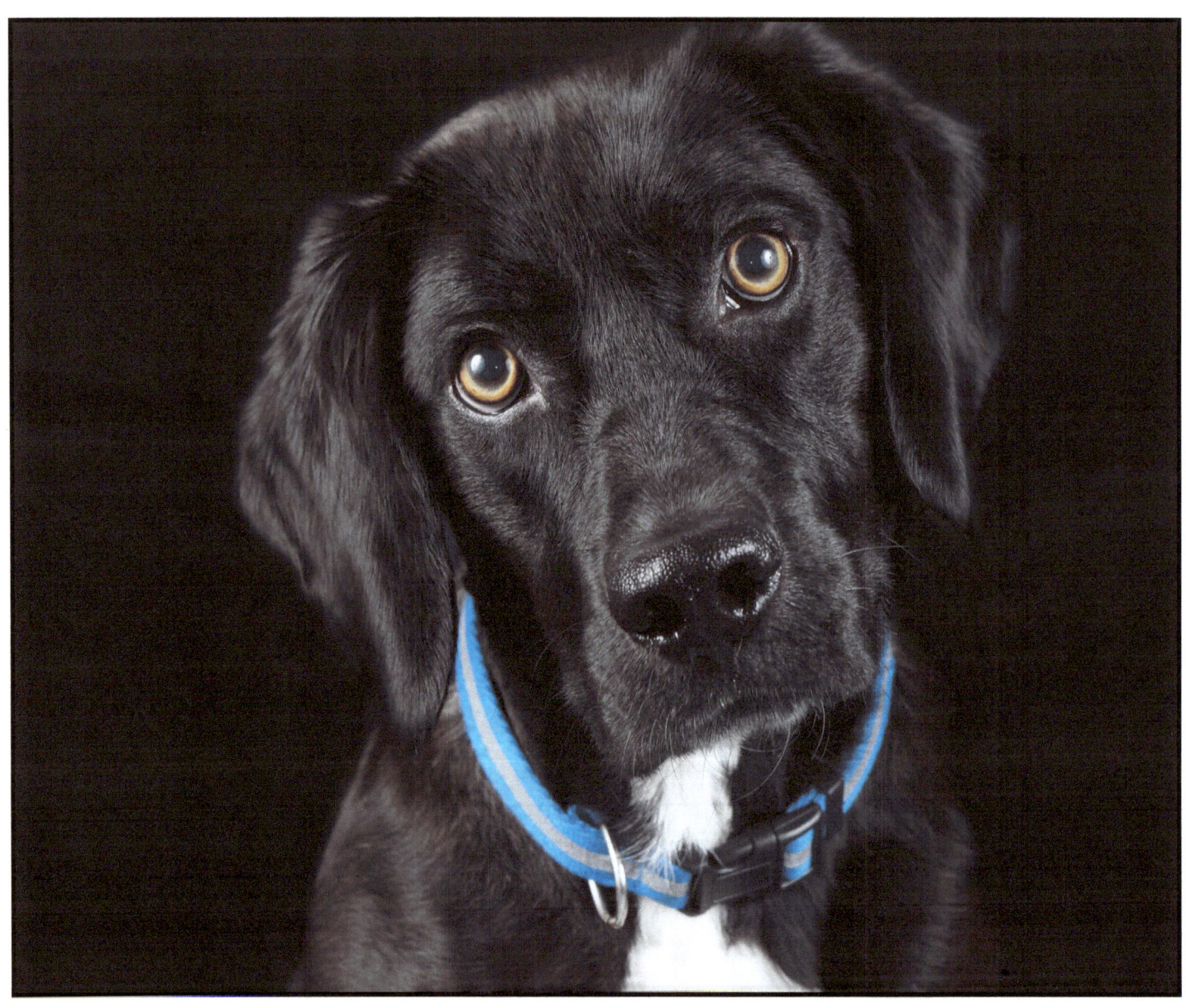

Wizard

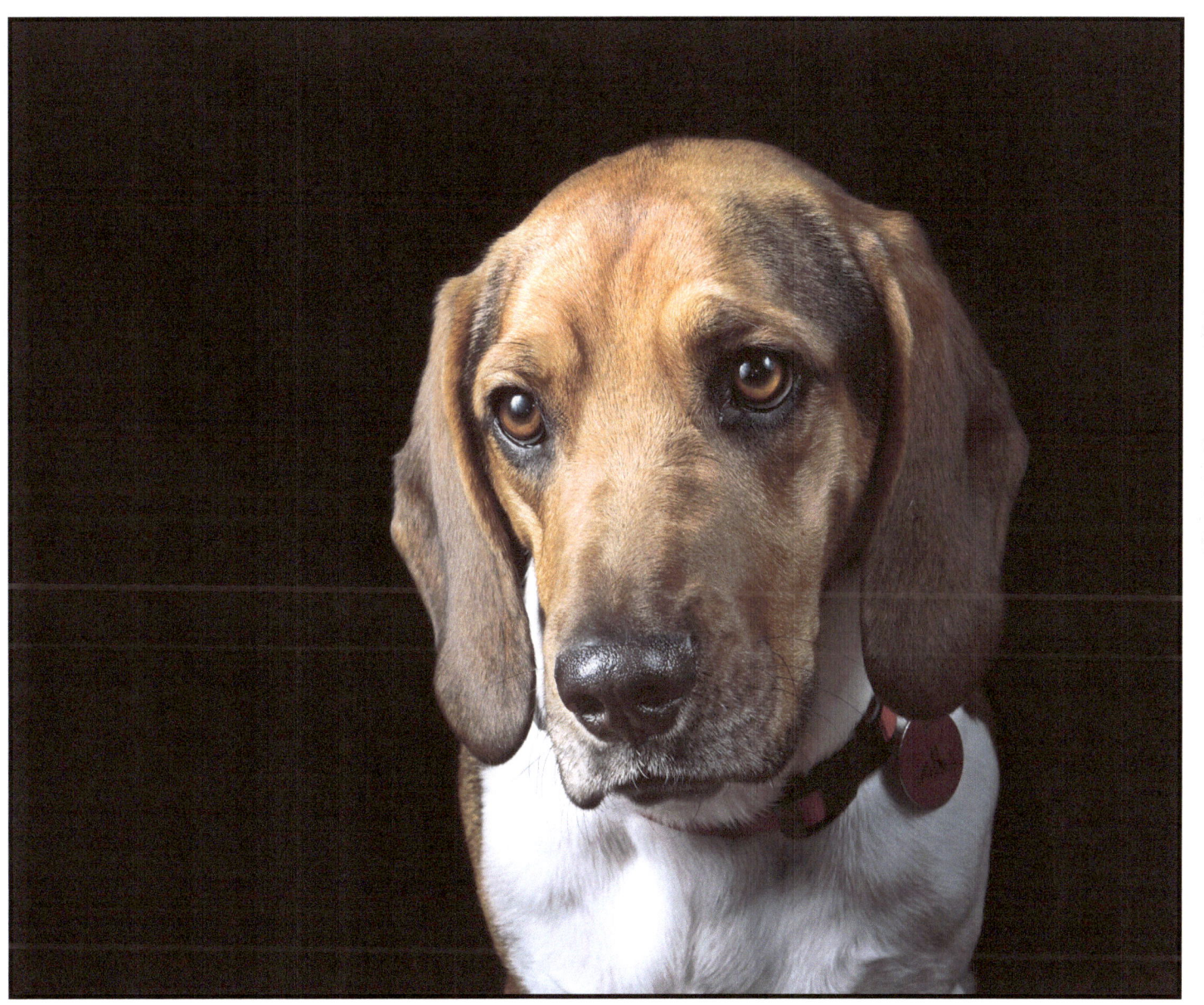

Dallas

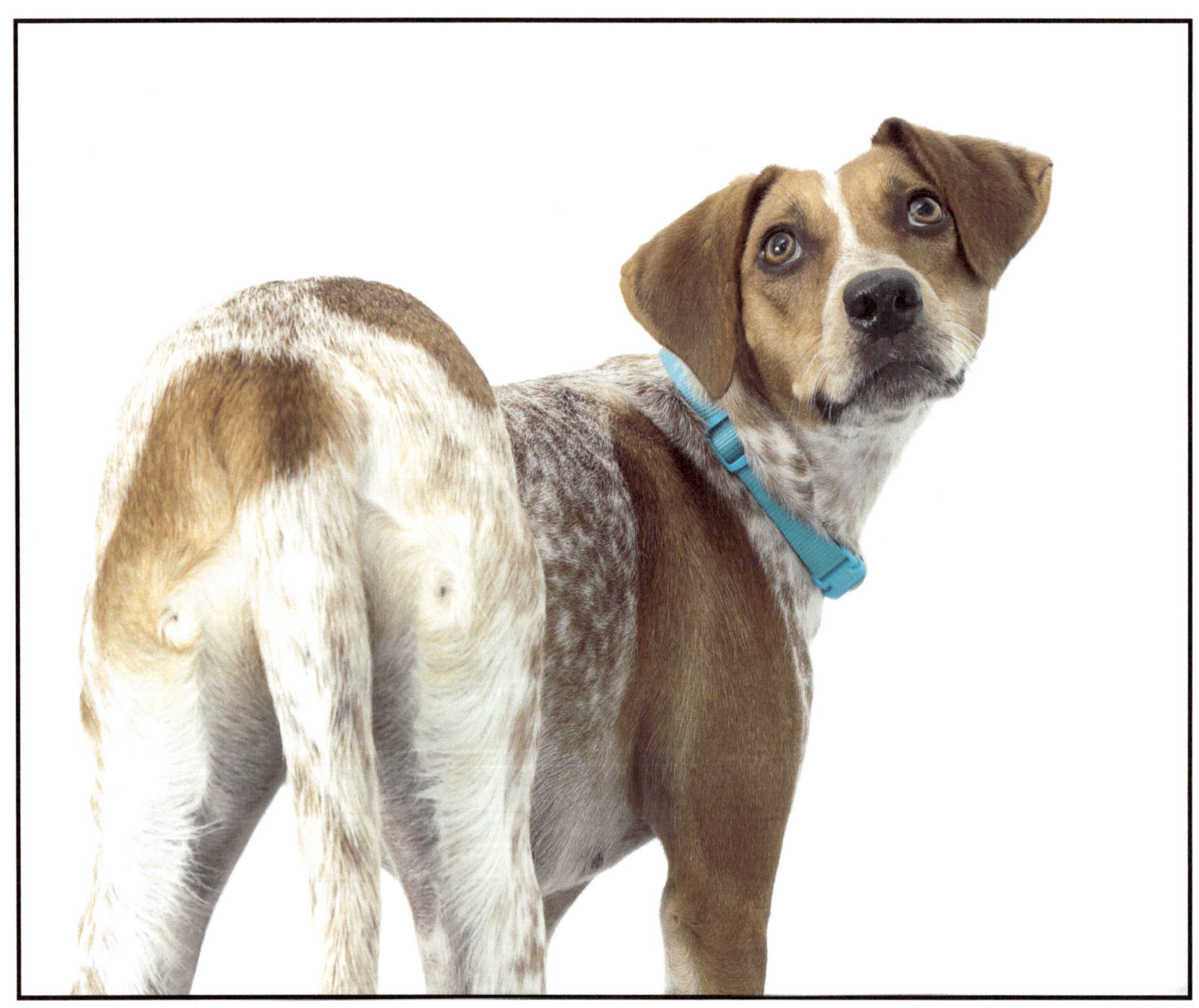

Shelby

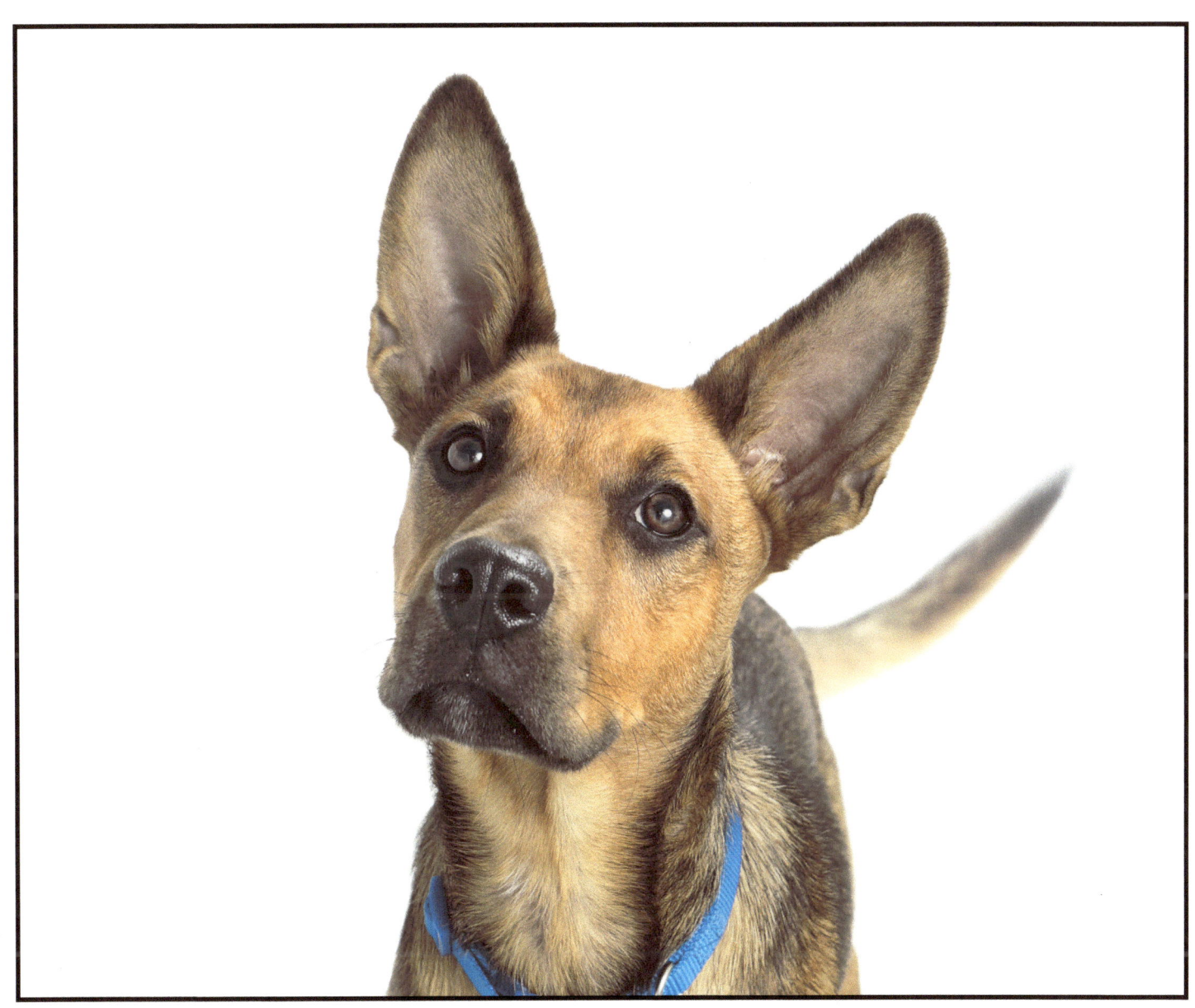

Rebel

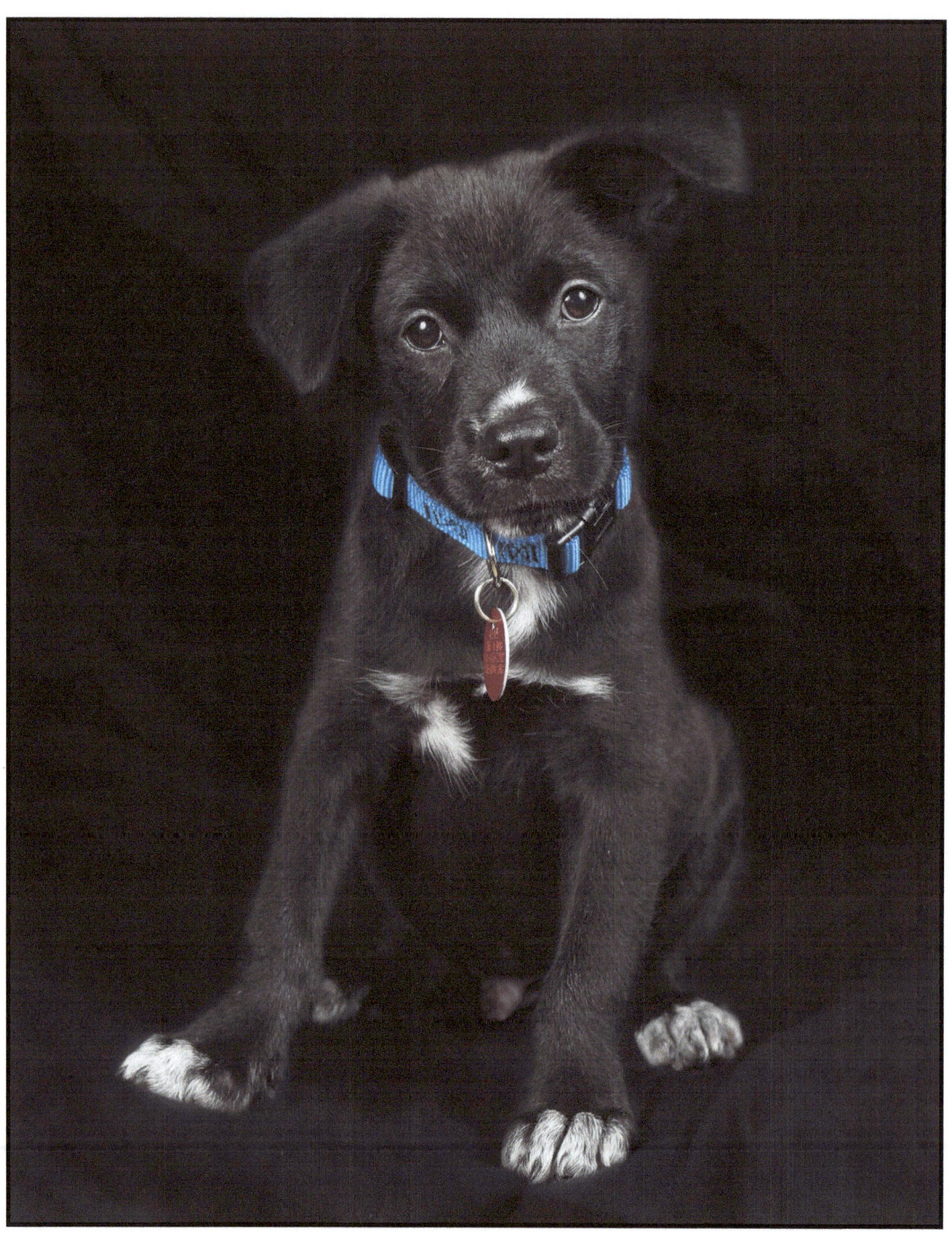

Mojo

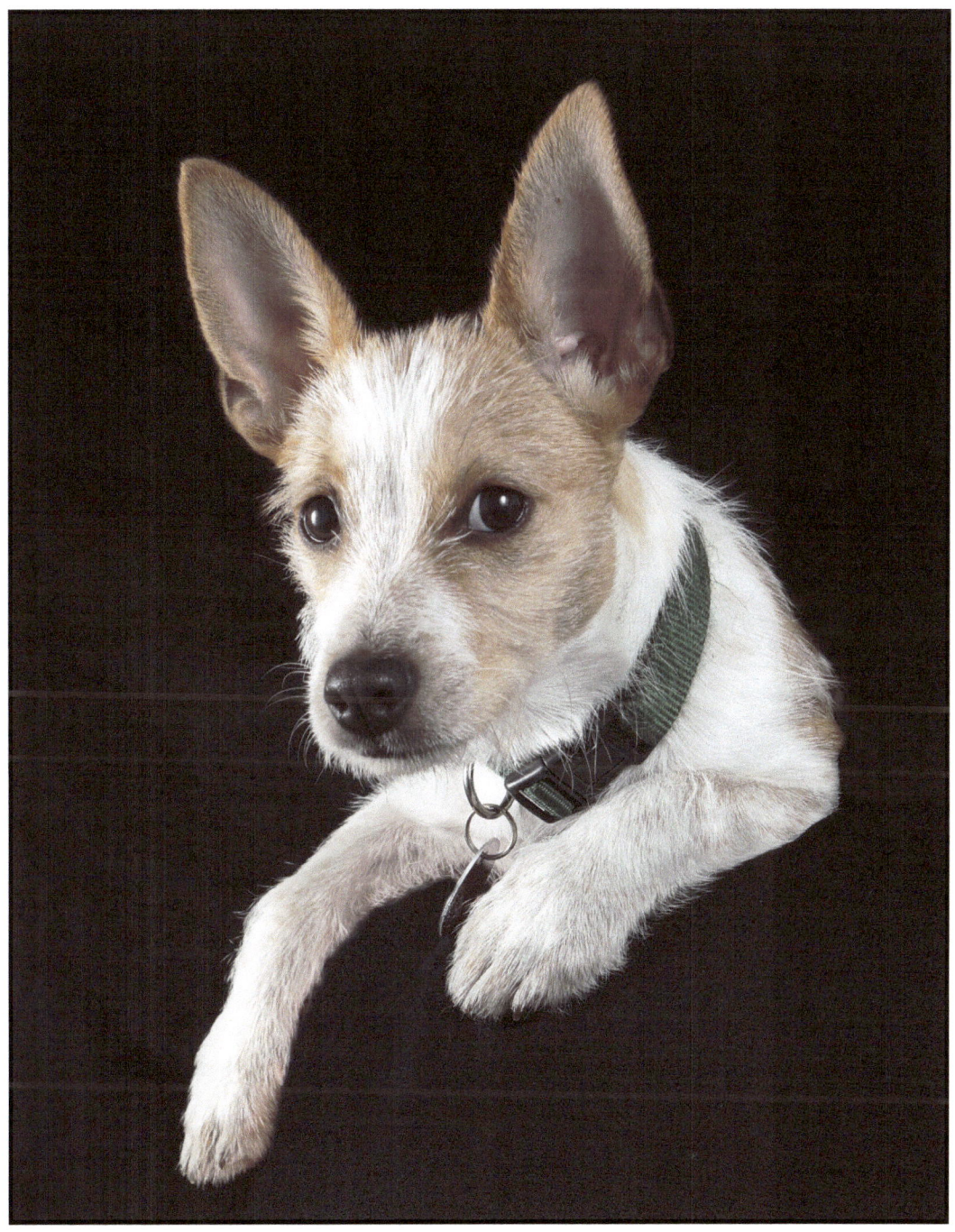

Luann

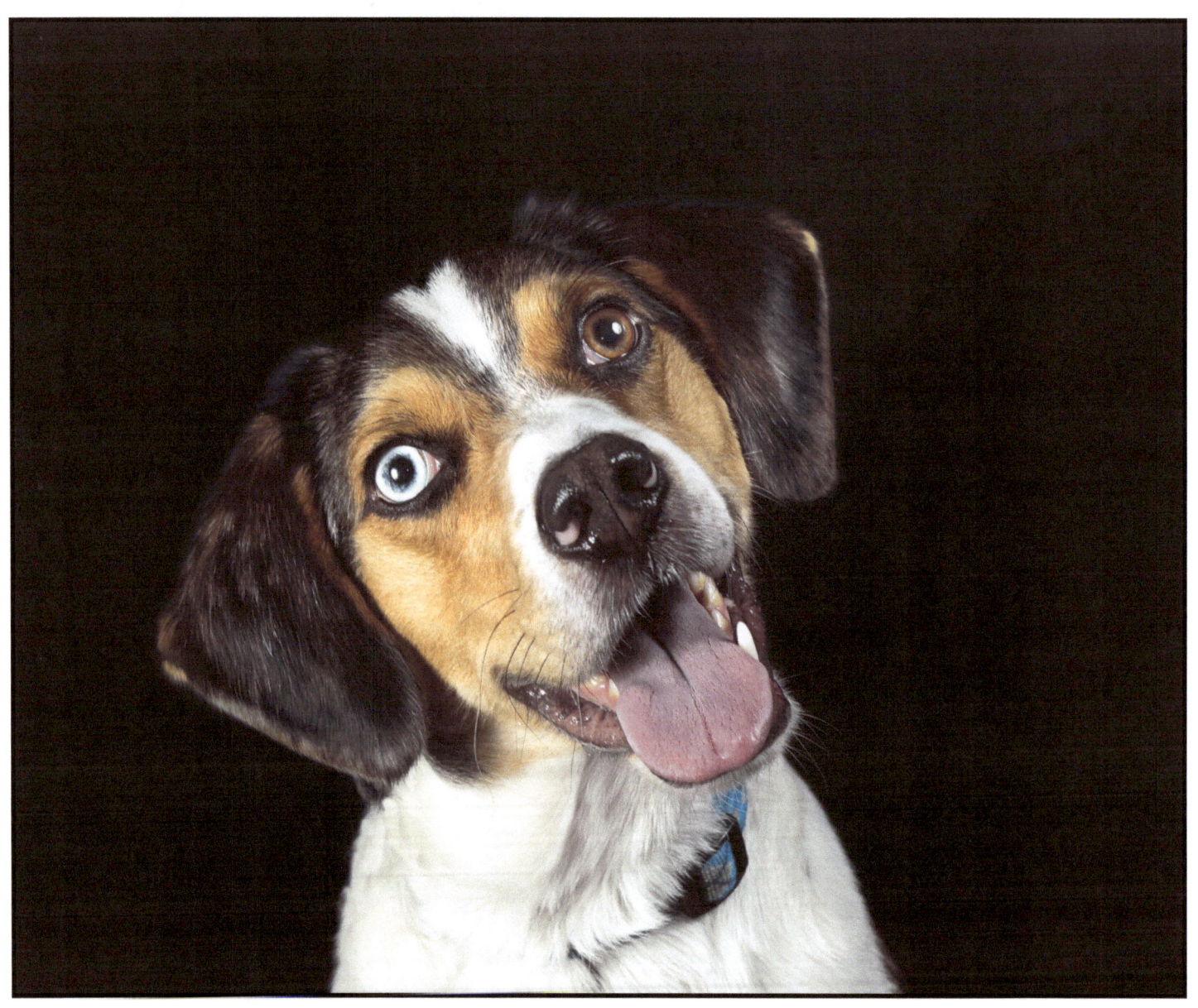

Mason

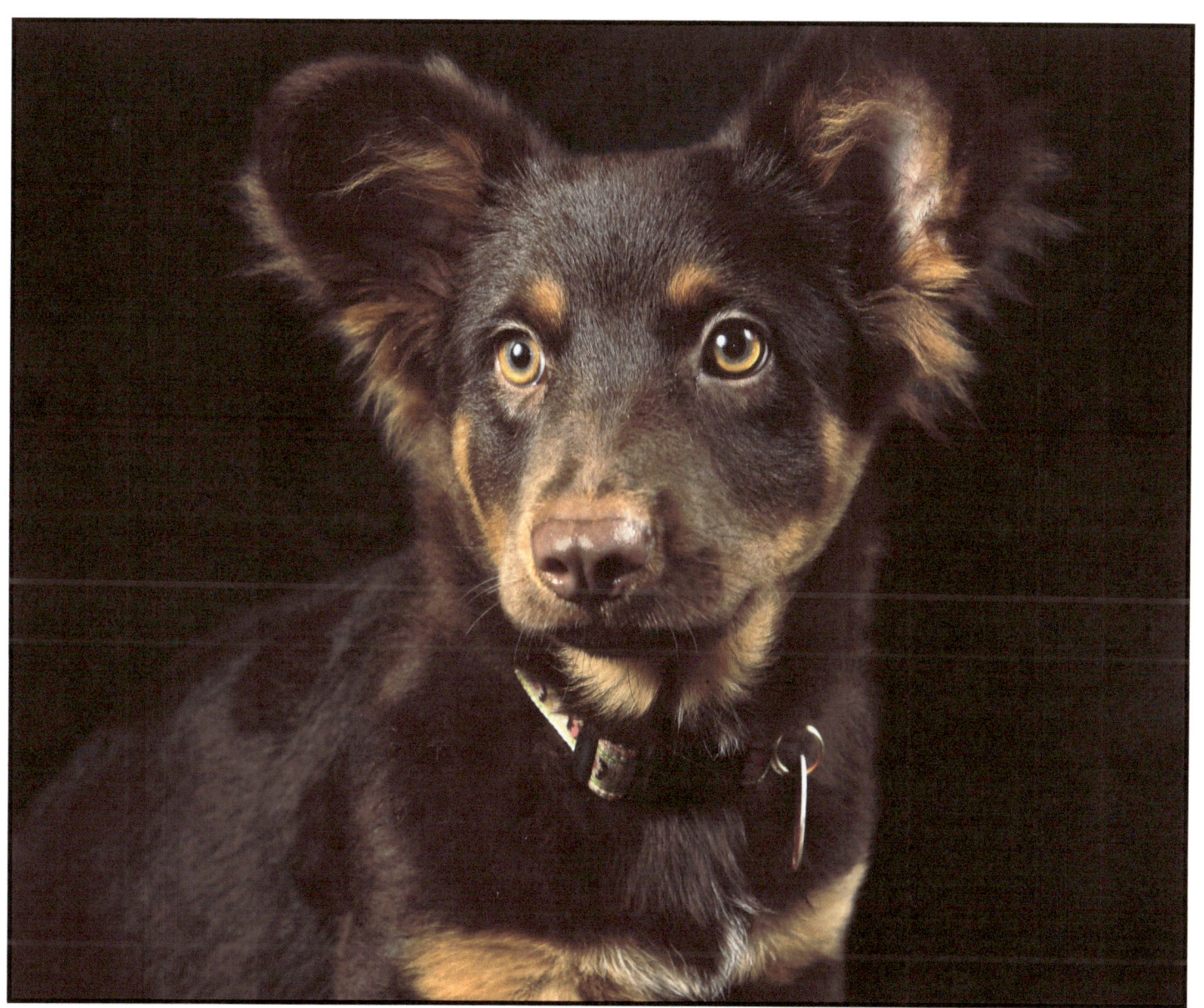

Cookie

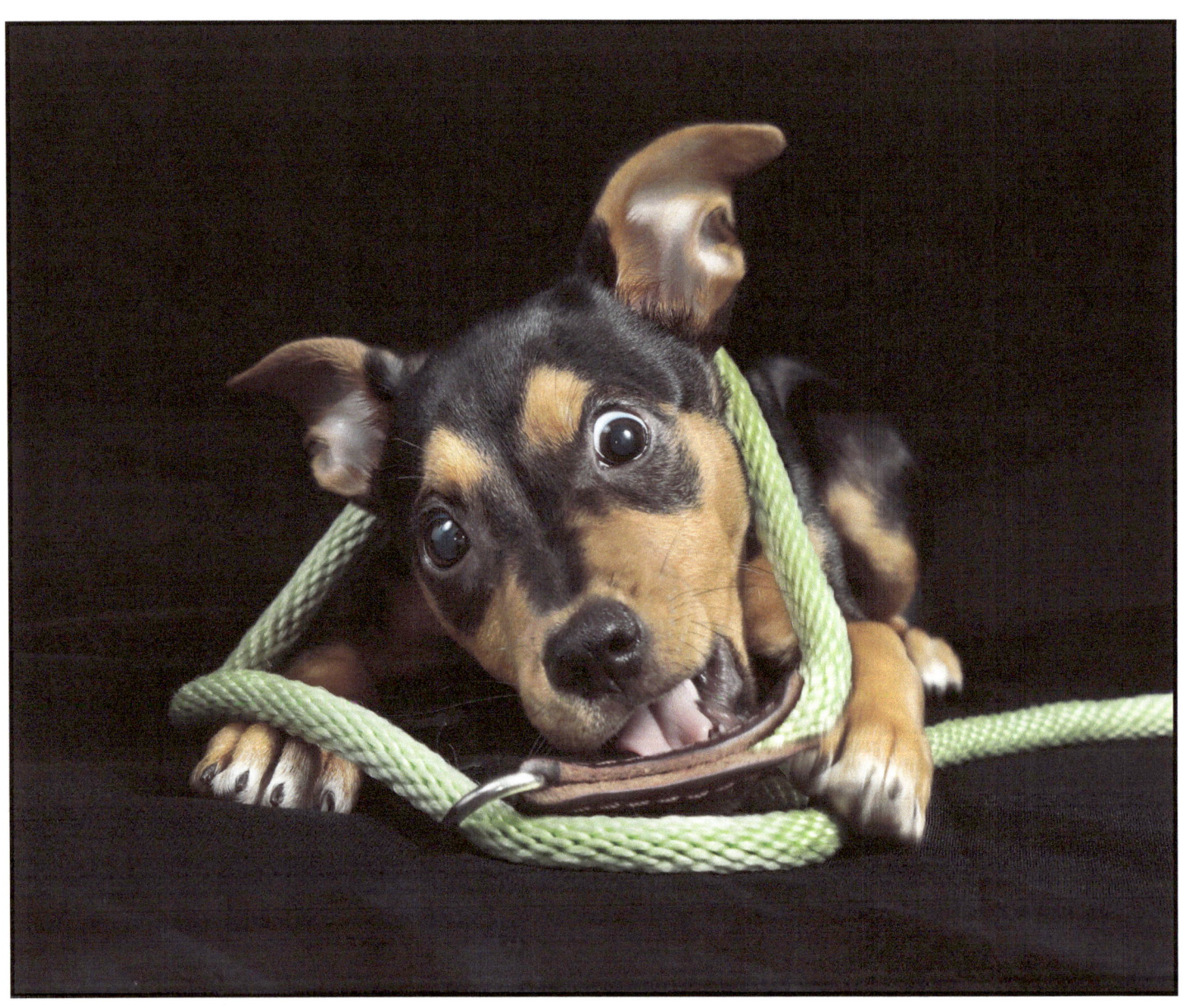

Jewel

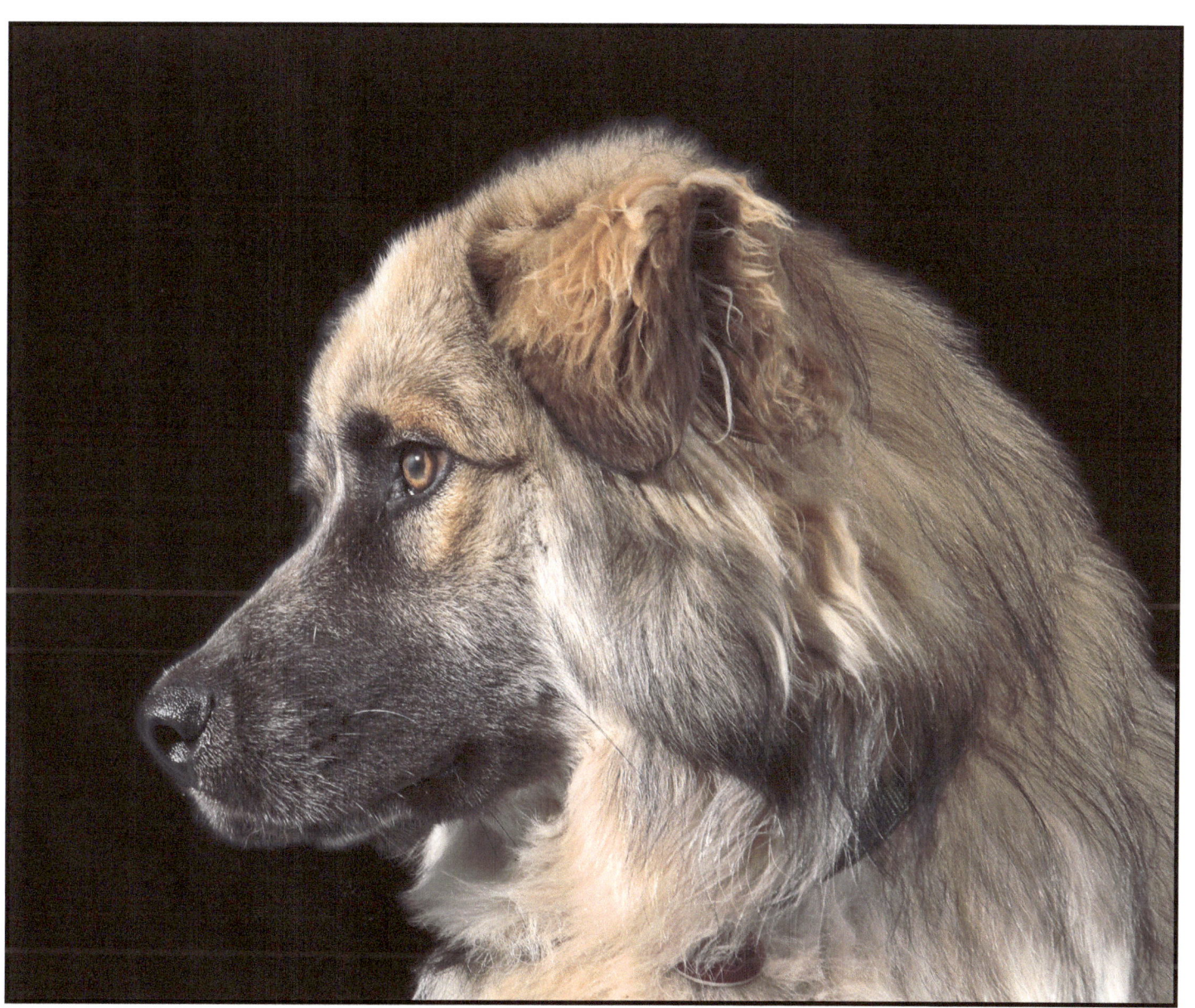

Buddy

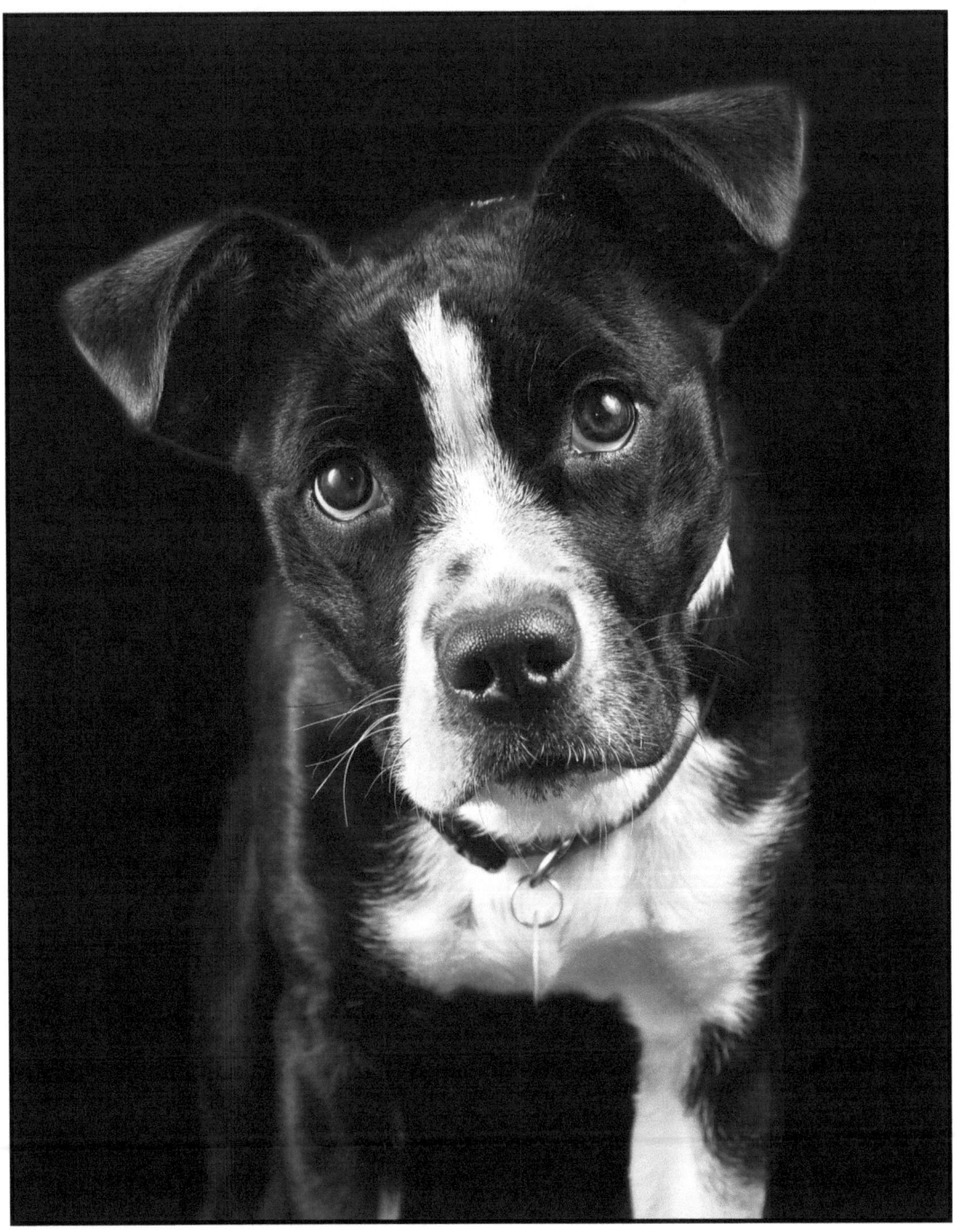

Zelda

Save A Dog, Inc. is a Massachusetts
based humane society whose focus
is abandoned dogs. They take in local
dogs of all breeds, sizes and shapes
who have become homeless for one
reason or another. The portraits in this
book are some of their rescues I've
been fortunate enough to photograph.

All images © Jay Sullivan 2014

Front Cover Photo: *Cocoa*
Back Cover: *Fresca*

eBooks available at Amazon and iTunes
or jayography.com